the hungry woman

the hungry woman

Cherríe L. Moraga
Afterword by Irma Mayorga

The Hungry Woman
A Mexican Medea

Heart of the Earth
A Popul Vuh Story

WEST END PRESS

An earlier version of *The Hungry Woman: A Mexican Medea* first appeared in *Out of the Fringe: Latino/a Theater and Performance*. María Teresa Marrero and Caridad Svich, eds. New York: Theater Communications Group, 2000.

Heart of the Earth: A Popol Vuh Story first appeared in *Puro Teatro: An Anthology of Latina Theater, Performance and Testimonios*. Alberto Sandoval and Nancy Saporta, eds. University of Arizona Press, 2000.

For more information on presenting *Heart of the Earth: A Popol Vuh Story,* utilizing the original puppetry, directed by Ralph Lee, contact The Mettawee River Company, 463 West Street, Apt. D 405, New York, NY 10014, 212-929-4777 (mettawee.org).

"Afterword: Homecoming," © 2001 by Irma Mayorga.

Printed in the United States of America

Fourth printing, January 2013
ISBN: 978-0-9705344-0-8

Book and cover design: Nancy Woodard

Front cover painting: *Omecihuatl,* watercolor on fiberglass paper, 22 x 30 inches, © 1979 Celia Herrera Rodríguez (celiaherrerar@aol.com)

West End Press • P.O. Box 27334 • Albuquerque, New Mexico 87125

Contents

Foreword

Hungry for God

Story

I remember that morning a year ago last summer when I pulled out from our household clothes dryer a full load of odd-looking dresses and skirts. I didn't recognize the sack shapes of plain rough fabric and worn cotton, with holes cut out for arms and head. They showed no signs of hemming, only a ribbon sewn in here and there for flourish. Whose dresses were they? Surely not my Linda's, whose adept hands could transform any rag into an art piece. Surely not my visiting stone-dyke pants-wearing comadre's. Then I recalled that la comadre had stopped here on her return from the Sun Dance and I suddenly saw that these dresses had been sewn by her own untutored butch hand. She had pledged to dance for four years, those four summers being the only time since the age of twelve when that militant macha would ever don a dress. And I thought, *she is just that hungry for god.*

After Reading Ofelia Zepeda

> Rain somewhere out in the desert.
> Comforted in this knowledge he turns over
> and continues his sleep.
> Dreams of women with harvesting sticks
> raised toward the sky.
> Ocean Power: Poems from the Desert

In the dream, I am to be initiated in a ceremony. We are many women from many nations. We prepare ourselves. We dress. I am nervous about what to wear, what is appropriate. There may be a test of some kind and I realize there are basic answers I have not memorized: basic elements of my cultura (the proper names for things, the language that comes with knowledge) that escape me.

With much difficulty, I try to tie up my hair. Its thin güera silkiness slips through fingers and hair pins. Somehow I manage to cover my head with a huipil and tie it awkwardly with a rose-colored string of Guatemalan cloth that I have gratefully recovered from Linda. She had been using it to bind her red medicine bundle, and I think of what strong prayers the string might carry from the contact.

I abandon my earlier anxieties as we begin to proceed into the arena, a rock-hard dirt field with a ceremonial structure at its center. Ironically, I feel a strange sense of correctness in my ill-fitting headdress, as it is a kind of "Chicana invention," I tell myself, drawing from many traditions. I am aware of the crowd of people watching me as I enter the ceremonial house, my compadre and his familia, and others who sit in the wooden bleachers that surround us. The house is a two-story wooden structure, narrow in depth, wide in length, like a kind of longhouse. A rickety set of exterior wooden stairs leads up to the second story, which is really no more than a platform where the initiation takes place out of view of the crowd. The highest part of stairway also extends into the structure. From there those of us waiting our turn to be initiated stand and observe the others. By the time I enter the landing, my headdress has fallen off. I feel freer, less encumbered, without it.

I watch the women before me, each in pairs, enact a simple ritual of inclusion into this extended nation of women. There is no test, I learn, overhearing the first set of questions proffered aloud and responded to. Each woman sits across from a kind of elder Maestra and each initiate, with few words spoken, is simply "brought in." That is my sense of it. When my turn arrives, Déborah, an O'odham woman I had met only weeks before, is my Maestra. We sit on our knees facing each other. Her manner is the calmness I remember in our first and only conversation as I dug up a young maguey on lodge grounds back home in Califas.

"Can I enter your space?" she asks me, meaning that corner of grounds where I am working. I stop digging.

"Yes, of course." I answer and wonder why she has taken the steps away from the others around the lodge to speak with me. My hand cups the top of the shovel handle. I lean into it.

She suggests to me that since we share ancestral ties to the same region, the Sonora Desert (Southern Arizona and Northern México), my herencia might also be O'odham. If so, her history is but a few month's stay away; mine spans almost a full century, when my grandparents first left Arizona for work in California.

"I've got to get back to the desert," she says. "Look how pale I am. If my relatives saw me now, they'd think I looked ill." Déborah is a deep rich brown color. It is I who pale in comparison. I marvel that she has taken the time to inquire about my ancestry, my maybe-Indianness. Me, not even quite convinced of my place in the circle of those mixed-blood lodge sisters, sitting and chatting softly on the other side of the grounds.

Now kneeling face to face with Déborah in ceremony, she exhibits the same generosity as in our first meeting. I don't remember what is said, only that she retains that same direct calmness in her approach to me, in her complete confidence in me. She places a simple cotton dress folded into a square into my arms. "It is for the sweatlodge," she tells me; and I am pleased to be given something that draws me more solidly into that circle, something more suitable than the mix of towels and knee-length tee-shirts and sheets of cloth I had been using. As we leave the ceremonial structure, I experience a profound sense of well-being, a full sense of belonging. My step meets the ground more solidly.

Suddenly, the ceremony is disrupted. A non-Native man wants to claim a rightful place in the ceremony. The scene suddenly becomes a kind of college campus where toddlers (white kids) require my attention. I am outraged by the situation in front of me, while at the same time sense, in the background, that my own blood child, who is not with me, is somehow endangered. The ceremony degenerates into estupideces and complete chaos. But upon awakening, the horror y lo ridículo of the dream's conclusion have little hold on me.

I awaken full of ceremony, like medicine. It is as close to joy as I can imagine.

In re-telling my dream, which was inspired by the writings of O'odham storyteller Ofelia Zepeda, I tell two stories, one inside the other: the dream-story of my own longings and fears as a mixed-blood xicanadyke living at the turn of the new century, and the story of my encounter with a could-be distant relative I had met a few years before. One story is lived while asleep and the other while awake. I've learned an enormous amount about my waking life from the uncensored stories my dreams tell. I tell my creative writing students, "Listen to them. Write them down. They are gifts from the gods."

In recent years, I've come to understand myth as a similarly divine(d) gift, an opening into the past, told in character and image, that can provide a kind of road map to our future. I am reminded here of the symbol for journey-ing employed by Meso-American scribes: little "patitas negras," black-inked and human-shaped footprints, marking out the road taken, traversing thou-sands of miles of desierto and montaña. This preoccupation with the past as a foretelling of our future may be the reason why I have lately begun to write stories placed in an imagined future. Like "a dream waiting to happen," I have written elsewhere.

Heart of the Earth and *The Hungry Woman* came to me as organic outgrowths of my own journeying as a xicanadyke and a writer in the early 80s. Rather belatedly in Movimiento terms, I first went south, as other Chicanos had before me, in search of my "raíces" and a cultural connection with a contemporary México. What I encountered instead was the daily, and often painful, reminder of my own cultural outsiderhood as a U.S.–born Mexican of mixed parentage. But the templos of México—Monte Albán, Palenque, Tulum, Teotihuacán—told me something different. As I ascended those temple steps, I unwittingly descended into the visceral experience of a collective racial memory that everything about my personal biography had rejected, but one that my writer's soul irrefutably embraced. It was as much the natural landscape in which those templos were placed, as the buried history contained within the structures, that brought a shudder of recognition to the surface of my skin: the green moss carpet on the steps of el Templo de la Cruz en Palenque; the crash of the Caribe against the walls of Tulum; the splice of sun illuminating the jeweled turquoise and jade of a Queztalcóatl relief in Teotihuacán. Those templos to the gods were the edification of a history lost to me. Thus began my (re)education process and my (re)turn to Mito in hunger for a true god and a true story of a people.

Who are my gods? Who are my people? The response is the same for both questions, I discovered, when I discovered the mutilated women of our indigenous american history of story: La Llorona, Coyolxauhqui, Coatlicue. I worship them in my attempt to portray them in all their locura, because I admire the living expression of their hungers. They, like my dreams, insist on truth and as such become my allies in a war against forgetfulness.

I write to remember—*is there no other way to say it?*—because I fear (and hope, in my cowardice) that I will die before any revolution is born blood-red on the horizon. I write to imagine, which is a way of remembering, as are dreams, that "we (women) were not always fallen from the mountain."

Imagine freedom, I tell myself. *Write freedom.* And I try to do so by painting pictures of prisoners on the page. They are the surviving codices of our loss. When you turn the page, those little five-toed footprints appear again in the spirit of the story. They are leading backwards, pointing toward a future of freedom.

Oakland, Califas
26 febrero 2001

the hungry woman
A Mexican Medea

Cherríe L. Moraga

Where can I go? Is it possible to imagine a world,
a time, where I would have a place?
There's no one I could ask. That's the answer.

Christa Wolfe, Medea: A Modern Retelling

For Marsha Gómez,
sculptor

1951–1998

The Hungry Woman: Development History

The Hungry Woman: A Mexican Medea was originally commissioned by Berkeley Repertory Theatre, where it received a staged reading on April 10, 1995, directed by Tony Kelly.

On December 2, 1995, the PLAY was presented in a staged reading as part of the Mark Taper Forum's New Works Festival in Los Angeles. It was directed by Lisa Wolpe.

As part of Theater Communications Group National Theater Artist Residency Program, funded by The Pew Charitable Trusts, *The Hungry Woman* was in development at The Brava Theater Center of San Francisco and received a staged reading on June 10, 1997, directed by the playwright.

On May 21, 1999, the PLAY was presented in a staged reading as part of A Contemporary Theater's/Hedgebrook Writers' Retreat Women's Playwright Festival in Seattle. It was directed by Richard E.T. White; Mame Hunt, Dramaturg.

The Esperanza Center and Guadalupe Cultural Arts Center of San Antonio, Texas presented the PLAY in a staged reading on February 20, 2000. It was directed by Irma Mayorga.

On December 4, 2000, *The Hungry Woman: A Mexican Medea* was presented as part of the Plays at the Border Festival at The Magic Theater of San Francisco. It was directed by the playwright.

Playwright's Note and Setting

The Time:
The early part of the second decade of the twenty-first century. A future I imagine based on a history at the turn of the century that never happened.

The Historical Place:
An ethnic civil war has "balkanized" about half of the United States into several smaller nations of people. These include: Africa-America located in the southern states of the U.S. (excluding, of course, Florida); the Mechicano Nation of Aztlán which includes parts of the Southwest and the border states of what was once Northern México; the Union of Indian Nations which shares, in an uneasy alliance with its Chicano neighbors, much of the Southwest and also occupies the Great Plains and Rocky Mountain regions; the Hawai'i Nation; and the confederacy of First Nations Peoples in the former state of Alaska.

The revolutionaries that founded these independent nations seceded from the United States in order to put a halt to its relentless political and economic expansion, as well as the Euro-American cultural domination of all societal matters including language, religion, family and tribal structures, ethics, art-making, and more. The revolution established economic and political sovereignty for seceding nations with the ultimate goal of defending aboriginal rights throughout the globe. Rebels scorned the ballot box and made alliance with any man or woman of any race or sexuality that would lift arms in their defense. When the Civil War was over, anyone, regardless of blood quantum, who shared political affinities with these independent nations was permitted to reside within their territories; however, the right to hold title to land was determined differently within each nation.

Several years after the revolution, a counter-revolution followed in most of the newly-independent nations. Hierarchies were established between male and female; and queer folk were unilaterally sent into exile.

The play takes place several years after MEDEA, who had served as a leader in the Chicano revolt, was exiled from Aztlán with her son, CHAC-MOOL, and her lesbian lover, LUNA. They reside in what remains of Phoenix, Arizona, located in a kind of metaphysical border region between Gringolandia (U.S.A.) and Aztlán (Mechicano country). Phoenix is now a city-in-ruin, the dumping site of every kind of poison and person unwanted by its neighbors. Scenes shift to the "present," where MEDEA is an inmate in a prison psychiatric ward, to events in the past leading up to MEDEA's incarceration. Psychiatric ward scenes are represented by a deadening silence and the glare of hospital lights. Phoenix is represented by the ceaseless racket of a city out of control (constant traffic, low-flying jet planes, hawkers squawking their wares, muy "Blade Runner-esque"). The lighting is urban neon. Most people look lousy in it.

Characters

MEDEA   A midwife and curandera in her late 40s.

LUNA   MEDEA's lover of seven years; stone mason and clay
                   sculptor, late 30s.

MAMA SAL   MEDEA's aging grandmother, 80s.

CHAC-MOOL   MEDEA's thirteen-year-old son.

CIHUATATEO (EL CORO):
      Chorus of four warrior women who, according to the Aztec myth,
      have died in childbirth. Here they are identified by the four directions
      and four primary Pre-Columbian colors: EAST (Red), NORTH
      (Black), WEST (White), and SOUTH (Blue). The figures wear the
      faces of the dead in the form of skulls. Their hands are shaped into
      claws. Their breasts appear bare and their skirts are tied with the
      cord of snake. They are barefoot, their ankles wrapped in shell
      rattles. The chorus performs in the traditional style of Aztec
      danzantes.

CIHUATATEO EAST   Also plays MEDEA's aging
                           PuertoRican caretaker in the
                           psychiatric hospital; wears red.

CIHUATATEO NORTH   Also plays PRISON GUARD,
                           TATTOO ARTIST and BORDER
                           GUARD; wears black.

CIHUATATEO WEST   Also plays LUNA's girlfriend,
                           African-American with Native ancestry;
                           wears white.

CIHUATATEO SOUTH   Also plays MEDEA's husband and
                           CHAC-MOOL's father; wears blue.

Act I

Prelude

> *[Pre-Columbian Meso-American music. The lights slowly rise on the altar to Coatlicue, the Aztec Goddess of Creation and Destruction. She is an awesome decapitated stone figure. She wears a serpent skirt and a huge necklace of dismembered hands and hearts, with a human skull at its center. THE CIHUATATEO flank her.]*

CIHUATATEO EAST:
> This is how all stories begin and end
> the innocence of an eagle feather
> stuffed inside a mother's apron.
>
> The birdboy growing there
> taking shape.
> The warrior son waiting in the wings
> taking flight.
>
> So, too begins and ends this story.
> The birth of a male child
> from the dark sea of Medea
>
> at the dawning of an age.
>
> *[CIHUATATEO NORTH crosses to CIHUATATEO EAST and hands her a red Nurse's cap. As she puts it on, NORTH covers her own face in a black ski mask.]*

NURSE: This is how all days begin and end.

Scene One

> [*PRISON GUARD stands upstage in ski mask, hands behind her back. A huge ring of jailer keys (very exaggerated) hangs from her military belt. There is a domino game set up nearby and an unmade hospital bed with a vase of wilting white flowers next to it. MEDEA is downstage, looking directly into the one-way mirror through which all activities in the psychiatric ward can be observed. Her dark hair is disheveled and her eyes are shadowed from lack of sleep. Still, MEDEA possesses a dark and brooding allure, akin to obsidian: a razor-sharp edge with a deep and lustrous sheen. MEDEA senses she is being watched.*]

PRISON GUARD: *(To audience)* A prison psychiatric hospital in the borderlands. The near future of a fictional past, dreamed only in the Chicana imagination.

> [*The PRISON GUARD crosses to MEDEA and hands her one of the flowers. She caresses it. NURSE enters with tray of food.*]

MEDEA: I have gone without campanitas on my kitchen table, I have gone without a kitchen table, a kitchen, a hearth for . . . how long has it been, Nurse?

NURSE: Many months.

MEDEA: Enough months to become years?

NURSE: Not yet.

MEDEA: Without a kitchen, my meals are brought to me on plastic trays, everything wrapped in plastic, the forks, the napkin, the salt and pepper, like on airplanes. I want to fly away.

> [*She lifts the lid to the food tray.*]

MEDEA: Is this soup?

NURSE: It's breakfast. We don't serve soup for breakfast.

MEDEA: *(Stirring it with her spoon)* It's gray soup.

NURSE: It's mush.

MEDEA: I like avena.

NURSE: Avena.

MEDEA: Oatmeal. It sticks to your ribs, like that commercial. *(Singing a little jingle)* "Sticks to your ribs all day."

NURSE: I remember that. *(Starts to exit.)*

MEDEA: You're leaving me?

NURSE: I got more patients than you. Eat your breakfast.

[NURSE exits.]

MEDEA: She's leaving me. Now I will have no one to talk to. I could talk to the man on the Quaker Oats box but she did not leave me the box or the man, just the mush. *(She pushes at it with her spoon.)* Avena. That's my baby's word. One of his first words because oatmeal was one of his first foods.

[She abandons the breakfast, crosses back to the wall of mirror, examines her face.]

MEDEA: I live inside the prison of my teeth. My voice can't escape this wall of maize-white tiles sealed shut. "Perfect masonry," Luna'd always say . . . about my teeth. I wish I had a mouth of corn, sweet baby corn. A mouth of baby teeth sucking at virgin purple pezones. How do I live now without her breasts? I can't open my mouth to suck her. Luna . . . ?

[Split-scene. LUNA's bedroom. Phoenix, early morning. The neon quality of the lighting and sudden rush of city sounds are distinct from the glaring bright lights and soundlessness of the psychiatric prison hospital. LUNA sits up in bed as awakened from a dream. The woman lying next to her under the covers, stirs.]

LUNA: To have somebody read your face in the light of day.

[LUNA *rises, dresses. Cross-stage NURSE reenters ward, removes the breakfast tray.*]

MEDEA: Cover the mirrors, Nurse. I don't want my son to see me like this, red-eyed, crows feet drooping. I am a motherless sight. Nurse, are you listening? Bring out the purple cloths. We'll pretend it is Lent and we await the resurrection of my son, my holy son. I'll sleep until then, until he returns to me. *(Pressing her face against the mirror)* The mirror is cold, impenetrable. You can never get inside it, unless you are a child or un muerto. I am neither, no longer, not yet. *(She spits at the mirrored wall. NURSE perfunctorily wipes it clean.)* Tiny ghosts live inside me. The ghost of my own pathetic girlhood. When I met Luna I imagined every touch was a gesture toward that girl-child.

NURSE: Tell your girlfriend, not me. She comes on Saturdays, three o'clock. Today is Friday. That's tomorrow. She's the one in the man's suit jacket who always comes with flowers. She's the face behind the flowers. You can't miss her.

MEDEA: But I do. I do miss my Luna.

NURSE: Why don't you tell her that when you see her? You never talk to her.

MEDEA: No. I only want to be an Indian, a Woman, an Animal in the Divine Ecosystem. The jaguar, the bear, the eagle.

[*The PRISON GUARD and NURSE begin to play dominoes.*]

MEDEA: *(At the mirror)* My chin is dropping, just like all the women in my family. My face is falling into my throat. Next thing I know I won't have a chin at all, just those thick necklaces of flesh strangling me. My eyelids are falling. One morning I'll open my eyes and the shades will be drawn permanently.

LUNA: Medea hid from the light. She always slept in the shadows, the windowless side of the bed, the shades drawn day or night. She slept with ear plugs, blindfolds.

MEDEA: I think it's the alcohol that sucks out all your juices, leaves you dry and black-eyed. The obsidian mirror and pulque. Vanity and drunkenness. The god's downfall and my own. I'm getting old. Old means the circles stay even after the cucumber peels.

NURSE: *(Mildly interested)* Cucumber peels?

MEDEA: You didn't know?

NURSE: What's to know?

MEDEA: During the day when Jasón was at work, I would lay my head down on the pillow and put the slices over my eyelids. They were so cool, one on each eye. I could hear Chac-Mool outside talking to the stonemason. It was paradise.

NURSE: The stonemason?

MEDEA: Yes. The woman, the migrant worker my husband Jasón hired to put in the garden patio.

[LUNA and CHAC-MOOL appear in MEDEA's memory.]

LUNA: You should plant corn.

CHAC-MOOL: My mom didn't say nothing about no corn.

LUNA: What's a garden without corn?

CHAC-MOOL: She's gonna plant medicine.

LUNA: Your mom makes medicine?

CHAC-MOOL: Yeah, she learned from my Bisabuela.

LUNA: Plant corn. A single corn plant can produce enough grain to feed a person for a day.

MEDEA: And the stonemason's voice entered me like medicine. Medicine for my brokenness.

[LUNA crosses back to bedroom, puts on a man's suit jacket.]

LUNA: I always liked that tiny fold hanging over Medea's eyes. It was like a delicate little awning, shading her from the world. I liked how that little mistake made her face less perfect. There's something to read in that. Nothing's printed in perfection. Only language I know is worry lines, a brow that looks like the valley floor in planting season. I'd trace my finger like a dumb plow along those furrows, but I could only guess at what Medea was thinking.

[LUNA bends down, kisses the woman beneath the bedcovers.]

LUNA: I'll be back tomorrow night. *(She gathers together a small bouquet of white cut flowers from the bedside.)* I am tired of mourning Medea. I dream of other women to bring moisture to places made dust by her departure.

[LUNA exits.]

Scene Two

[PRISON GUARD and NURSE push MEDEA's hospital bed to a cramped government-funded urban apartment. The GUARD dumps a load of trash around the floor: old magazines, used tissues, newspapers, junk mail, a few empty pints of booze.]

PRISON GUARD: *(To the audience)* One year earlier. The land of the exiled. Phoenix, Arizona. What never rose up from the ashes of destruction.

[S/he hands a letter to MEDEA and exits. MEDEA paces back and forth with the letter in one hand and a bottle of tequila in the other. LUNA is on her knees with a wastebasket, picking up the trash that has just been dumped on the floor.]

MEDEA: He writes me in fucking lawyerese. I hate that! Fucking lawyer, fucking poet-lawyer! There ought to be a law against fucking with language that way. Mira esta mierda. *(She thrusts the letter at LUNA.)*

LUNA: I've seen the letter, Medea.

[Cross-stage CIHUATATEO SOUTH appears as JASÓN. He wears military blue.]

MEDEA/JASÓN: "She reminds me of you, Medea. Your once-innocence. Your wide-eyed eagerness. She is the Medea you were before the war, before 'politics' changed you . . . changed us."

MEDEA: ¡Pendejo! She's a virgin, sabes? Bueno . . . *was* a virgin.

LUNA: The bride-to-be? I thought they didn't make virgins no more.

MEDEA: She's nineteen years old.

LUNA: Oh. How does he know for sure?

MEDEA: That she's nineteen?

LUNA: That she's a virgin.

MEDEA: She bled for him.

LUNA: He wrote you that?

MEDEA: Uh-huh.

LUNA: Grosero.

JASÓN: "She bled for me, just as you did once."

MEDEA: *(To JASÓN)* Ay, Jasóncito, that was a wound you found too many years ago, a bleeding ulcer between my legs.

[MEDEA crumples up the letter and tosses it on the ground. LUNA picks it up, puts it in the trash. JASÓN exits.]

MEDEA: "Politics." Men think women have no love of country, that the desire for nation is a male prerogative. So like gods, they pick and choose who is to be born and live and die in a land I bled for equal to any man. Aztlán, how you betrayed me! Y acá me encuentro in this wasteland where yerbas grow bitter for lack of water, my face pressed to the glass of my own revolution like some húerfana abandonada.

LUNA: You aren't an orphan, Medea.

MEDEA: I have no *mother*land. Can you stop doing that? *(The cleaning.)*

15

LUNA: It bothers you?

MEDEA: Yes.

LUNA: It bothers me, too.

[*MEDEA sloshes tequila onto the floor. With intention.*]

MEDEA: I need to talk to you.

[*LUNA stops.*]

LUNA: Are you jealous?

MEDEA: No, not jealous.

LUNA: Medea.

MEDEA: I'm a rabid dog.

LUNA: You've never divorced Jasón . . . why?

MEDEA: You believe in that piece of paper?

LUNA: Yes, when it means you could be taken away from me.

MEDEA: I'm not your custody case. Don't treat me like one.

LUNA: No, Chac-Mool is. Our son is the custody case.

MEDEA: My son.

LUNA: Why don't you get dressed and go to work?

MEDEA: Work! I suck off the seven-pound creations of other women!
That's all. I catch their babies and throw them back at them.

LUNA: Just get dressed. *(Starts to exit.)*

MEDEA: Jasón doesn't need Chac-Mool now. He'll get his progeny. The
teenager waifa will see to that.

LUNA: She's Indian?

MEDEA: Indian enough. And young enough. She'll have a litter of breed-babies for him.

LUNA: He's getting old, Medea. He wants Chac-Mool.

MEDEA: He hasn't asked for him.

LUNA: The boy's turning thirteen, he has the right to decide for himself.

MEDEA: No.

LUNA: Medea.

MEDEA: There's time yet.

LUNA: For what?

MEDEA: I don't know. Something.

LUNA: I always thought that if Jasón had felt even the smallest part of what I've come to feel for Chac-Mool, that he never would've let him go. He would have held him kicking and screaming to his chest. He would've forced you to choose.

MEDEA: Lucky for you he didn't.

LUNA: That's what I thought.

MEDEA: Didn't you hear? Jasón wants a divorce. I'm yours forever. Happy?

[MAMA SAL enters, laden with a heavy leather satchel.]

LUNA: *(Taking satchel from her.)* Lemme help you.

MAMA SAL: Gracias, hija. Am I . . . ?

LUNA: *(To MEDEA)* Nah, I'm on my way out.

[LUNA exits. MEDEA drops back into bed.]

MEDEA: *(To self)* And our hands are left empty . . . she and I, childless women que chupamos each other's barren breasts?

MAMA SAL: You're gonna push her so far away from you, she won't be able to find her way back.

MEDEA: Good. She's a liability.

MAMA SAL: ¿Por qué hablas así?

MEDEA: I can't bring her into this. It'll make things worse.

MAMA SAL: They can't get worse, Medea. We lost it all already, ¿no recuerdas?

MEDEA: Not my son. I didn't lose my son.

MAMA SAL: Levántate. La clínica's got two women in labor.

MEDEA: No puedo. You go for me instead.

MAMA SAL: Ay, Medea. I've burped every border baby from here to Nogales already today.

MEDEA: No puedo.

MAMA SAL: Medea, you got to get back to work.

MEDEA: I don't trust myself. I feel my hands as liquid as the river.

MAMA SAL: La poet. It's your mind that's liquid from tanta tequila.

> [*MAMA SAL rummages through her satchel pulling out small sacks of yerbas. She hands MEDEA a few clear capsules of ground herb.*]

MAMA SAL: Ten.

MEDEA: What are they?

MAMA SAL: Tómalos and not with the tequila.

[MEDEA pops the capsules into her mouth.]

MAMA SAL: Now, sleep it off.

[MAMA SAL closes up her satchel and exits.]

Scene Three

> *[CHAC-MOOL sits beneath a glaring spotlight. It looks like an interrogation room. Various small rings of silver hang from his eyebrow, ear, lip and nose. The TATTOO ARTIST, who is the PRISON GUARD wearing a worker's apron, blindfolds CHAC-MOOL with a black bandanna. CHAC-MOOL offers his shoulder as TATTOO ARTIST begins to etch out with a needle the first markings of the tattoo.]*

TATTOO ARTIST: What's the matter? Why are you covering your eyes?

CHAC-MOOL: To see.

TATTOO ARTIST: To see what?

CHAC-MOOL: The swirls of purple and forest green. If I cover my eyes, I am asleep in a dream. I can dream anything I want. At night, before I dream, I stay up and watch the moon cross the sky. Each night it's a long journey, unless you forget to watch her. Then she can appear in completely different places as if by magic. Have you seen the moon the last four nights? The evening moon?

TATTOO ARTIST: I think so.

CHAC-MOOL: What did you see?

TATTOO ARTIST: A sliver.

CHAC-MOOL: A sliver in the smoggy haze?

TATTOO ARTIST: . . . Yeah.

CHAC-MOOL: A thin brush stroke in the sky. One delicate turn of a silver-haired paintbrush marking the sky with her hue.

TATTOO ARTIST: You talk beautiful for a boy.

CHAC-MOOL: At sunrise, she melts from the sun's glow. Soft, insistent.

TATTOO ARTIST: You watch her all night?

CHAC-MOOL: La luna? Yes, like a lover. *(To himself)* "The Boy Who Fell in Love with the Moon."

TATTOO ARTIST: What do you know about love? You're too young.

CHAC-MOOL: I am a boy who sleeps alone in his pijamas and wakes up in the middle of the night wishing for something.

TATTOO ARTIST: What? Manhood?

CHAC-MOOL: No. Full-grown innocence. Such lightness of flesh that I could rise above my bed and fly to the moon. I believed that once, pumping my swing harder and harder, I believed I could touch la luna. My mom sang me songs of flying to the moon as she pushed my back.

[*Singing*]

"Up in a balloon, boys, up in a balloon.
Sailing 'round the little stars and all around the moon."

It seemed possible then.

TATTOO ARTIST: And now?

CHAC-MOOL: Now I know more and my dreams are getting as heavy as my heart.

TATTOO ARTIST: Pity.

CHAC-MOOL: Don't pity me. Pity my mother. She sleeps during the day when la luna has disappeared to the other side of the earth. She can't stand the relentless sun without her, she says. She can't stand the brilliant productiveness of the day.

TATTOO ARTIST: *(Cutting deeper into the skin)* Cover your eyes.

[*CHAC-MOOL, puts a hand over his blindfold, wincing as THE TATTOO ARTIST pierces.*]

CHAC-MOOL: I don't remember if this is the right way to pray. I was never officially taught. It is not allowed. Everything relies on memory. We no longer have any records, nothing is written down. But I heard. I heard about Aztlán and the piercing of the skin as a prayer.

TATTOO ARTIST: You think that's what you're doing, praying? You think this is holy, driving needles into the paper of your flesh? Hanging metal off your eyebrows, your nostrils, your lips?

CHAC-MOOL: I pray as you cut. I pray deep and hard and if it pusses, I pray harder for the pain. In the center of pain, there is always a prayer. A prayer where you get up to leave and a whole army of people is there to carry you away. You aren't alone anymore.

TATTOO ARTIST: Is this what they're teaching kids now in this ghetto?

CHAC-MOOL: They don't know what to teach us no more. We only get what's left over.

TATTOO ARTIST: (*Pulling the blindfold off of CHAC-MOOL*) "What's Left Over."

[*NURSE appears upstage in the corner, spinning a bingo machine.*]

NURSE: B-7!

MAMA SAL (*Entering*): Bingo!

[*The TATTOO ARTIST rolls CHAC-MOOL over to the "game room," hands him a bingo card and a handful of pinto beans for markers. MAMA SAL and SAVANNAH and CIHUATATEO SOUTH are already busy at the game. The TATTOO ARTIST joins in.*]

NURSE: N-33!

MAMA SAL: By the time I was born, communism had spread all over the world. The Jews and the italianos had already brought it over in boats to América. . . . Are you taking notes, Chaco?

CHAC-MOOL: Yes. *(Indicates "mental ones.")*

MAMA SAL: But it didn't catch on until it went south . . . a Cuba, El Salvador, a Nicaragua. Then the Cold War thawed and all the small commie countries began to dissolve también.

SAVANNAH: Except for Cuba.

MAMA SAL: Of course, except for Cuba. He knows that!

NURSE: G-52.

MAMA SAL: In the melt-down, la política changed completely, and the only thing los gringos cared about was the language you used, the bible you carried, y la lana que tenía en tu pocket.

SAVANNAH: And that you weren't sticking your hand into theirs.

CHAC-MOOL: Is this the official version?

NURSE: N-31.

MAMA SAL: Yes. I was there.

CHAC-MOOL: You're editorializing, 'buela. I just need the facts.

MAMA SAL: There are no facts. It's all just story.

CHAC-MOOL: Fine.

MAMA SAL: Pues, all this born-again-christian-charismatic-apocalyptic-eucalyptus-que-sé-yo gave fresh blood a la práctica de nazism y la plática de—

SAVANNAH: Wetback go home.

NURSE: B-5.

MAMA SAL: Mientras cancer clustered through every Mechicano farm town and low-income urban neighborhood en Gringolandia. Pesticides poured down like rain upon los trabajadores and into the water system.

SAVANNAH: There were no protections. Maquildoras sprang up all along the entire border. Babies were being born without brains. And Mexico became a Puerto Rico overnight.

NURSE: I-24.

MAMA SAL: Los transnational corporate patrones had turned the whole global economy—

SAVANNAH: Unionized jobs, environmental protection, public health and safety standards, a living wage—

MAMA SAL: Into a poisoned alphabet soup.

SAVANNAH: NAFTA, the WTO, GATT, and FTAA.

MAMA SAL: So, as you can already imagine Castro began to despair y tengo que decir que . . . me, too. I figured if Fidel goes, it's all over for the rest of us.

SAVANNAH: It was only a matter ot time.

NURSE: G-46.

MAMA SAL: Tu mamá y su cadre were one among many small groups organizing revolts in pueblitos throughout the Southwest. Then Los Independentistas declared Vieques Island free and sovereign—

SAVANNAH: Which inspired an international response, already spear-headed by the Mayas in Chiapas.

CHAC-MOOL: The Zapatistas.

NURSE: O-69.

MAMA-SAL: The Zapatistas took on the PRI and the PAN y hasta el partido de la TORTILLA and the Mexican president got shot and bueno . . . the rest is history. Pan-indigenismo tore América apart and Aztlán was born from the pedacitos.

SAVANNAH: Uniting the dinenfranchised diaspora of Indian-mestizos thrughout the Southwest.

MAMA-SAL: We were contentos for awhile—

SAVANNAH: Sort of. Until the revolutionaries told the women, put down your guns and pick up your babies.

MAMA-SAL: ¡Fuera de las calles!

SAVANNAH: And into the kitchens! *(Beat)* Now that's not in the "official" version.

NURSE: I-18.

MAMA SAL: Just like the Gringo and Gachupín before them.

SAVANNAH: And then en masse, all the colored countries—

MAMA SAL: Threw out their jotería.

SAVANNAH: Queers of every color and shade and definition.

MAMA SAL: Y los homos became peregrinos . . . como nomads, just like our Aztec ancestors a thousand years ago.

NURSE: B-11.

SAVANNAH: And we made a kind of gypsy ghetto for ourselves in what was once a thriving desert.

MAMA SAL: They call it "Phoenix," pero entrenos, we name it "Tamoanchán," which means—

CHAC-MOOL: "We seek our home."

MAMA SAL: And the seeking itself became home.

NURSE: 0-75.

CHAC-MOOL: Luna told me they just finished building a strip of casinos along Cuahtemoc Boulevard.

MAMA SAL: Casinos? In Aztlán?

CHAC-MOOL: With neon, glitter and the works.

SAVANNAH: I guess they figure the Indians are making a killing on gambling throughout the Union, why not the Chicanos, too? No one's gonna leave them in the dust of socialism.

MAMA SAL: Wannabes. First it's the sweat lodge, then the sundance. Ni saben su propia tradición indígena.

NURSE: G-47.

MAMA SAL: Still, maybe it's not such a bad thing. Our people is already crazy for the (*Slapping down the last bean*) Bingo!

SAVANNAH: No way! Again!

CHAC-MOOL: Ah, man! And I was almost there!

SAVANNAH: Damn!

[*Black out*].

Scene Four

[*CHAC-MOOL, shirtless in overalls, and LUNA can be seen working in a small urban garden (a barely redeemable abandoned lot bordering their building). City noises persist. LUNA digs at the ground with a long-handled hoe.*]

LUNA: After the first rains the planting begins. You burn incense at the four corners of the field. Smoke the seed to be planted with copal and candles. You fast.

CHAC-MOOL: For how long?

LUNA: Seven days is good. I would do seven days.

CHAC-MOOL: Seven days.

LUNA: The first three are the hardest, after that you're high. *(He smiles.)* You don't miss eating, really. Then you place candles at the four points, the four corners.

CHAC-MOOL: I feel like everybody's gonna know stuff I don't know.

LUNA: You know enough. When you harvest the maíz, the ears are broken from the plants in the field. You should bring them back to the house in a basket. The ears are then tied together or braided into clusters. Then they are hung up to dry, separated by color.

CHAC-MOOL: Blue, black, red, white—

LUNA: When you find twin ears, one is kept for seed, the other offered to Tonantzín.

[MEDEA enters. CHAC-MOOL spies her.]

CHAC-MOOL: Luna . . .

LUNA: The shelled grain is mixed together again for planting.

MEDEA: Once you're initiated, you have to leave for good. You know that.

CHAC-MOOL: Mom.

MEDEA: Thank you, Luna, for respecting my wishes.

LUNA: I—

CHAC-MOOL: She didn't do nothing, Mom. I asked her to teach me.

MEDEA: And I asked her to wait.

CHAC-MOOL: Mom, I turn thirteen in the Spring.

MEDEA: Everybody seems to think that I have forgotten when your birthday is. I know when your birthday is. I was there for the first one, remember?

CHAC-MOOL: Why you getting so pissed off?

MEDEA: This is not a game, Chac. A get-back-to-your-raíces-harvest-moon-ritual.

LUNA: That's not fair, Medea.

MEDEA: Fair? Who's the real warrior here, Luna? You or me? Show me your scars.

[*MEDEA thrusts both arms out at LUNA to reveal a trail of scars from shoulder to wrist bone.*]

LUNA: Mine don't show. You win. (*Handing CHAC-MOOL the hoe*) Here, Chac. We'll finish later.

CHAC-MOOL: Luna . . .

LUNA: It's okay.

[*She exits.*]

CHAC-MOOL: Mom.

MEDEA: What?

CHAC-MOOL: I'm gonna go back to Aztlán, and make 'em change, Mom. You'll see. Like those Cuban kids who went back to Cuba in the 70s and became Castro sympathizers.

MEDEA: Who told you about that?

CHAC-MOOL: Bisabuela. Except the revolutionaries, I mean the people who call themselves revolutionaries, like my Dad. . . . They're the traitors to the real revolution. And I'm gonna—

MEDEA: What?

CHAC-MOOL: . . . Make them see that.

MEDEA: You are?

CHAC-MOOL: You'll see.

MEDEA: Did Luna tell you it was four years? Four years of Sundance until you can even visit us again.

CHAC-MOOL: No.

MEDEA: That's a long time, Chac-Mool.

CHAC-MOOL: I guess I really didn't think about that part.

MEDEA: Your father hasn't asked for you to come back, you know.

CHAC-MOOL: But I thought he wrote you.

MEDEA: He's getting married.

CHAC-MOOL: Oh.

MEDEA: To an Apache. He's thinking of other things right now. He's thinking of her.

CHAC-MOOL: Is she gonna have a baby?

MEDEA: Not yet.

CHAC-MOOL: He's an old man, Mom. I mean, to get married again.

MEDEA: Men are never old, Chac-Mool.

[*MEDEA looks up to the evening sky. CHAC-MOOL watches her.*]

MEDEA: If your father comes to get you and he could come at any time, you have to know for sure what you want. You can't change your mind. He has the right to take you, but only if you agree to go.

CHAC-MOOL: And if I don't go?

MEDEA: You don't get another chance.

CHAC-MOOL: But Mom, I don't know.

MEDEA: I know.

[Pause. CHAC-MOOL goes to MEDEA. She wraps her arms around him.]

MEDEA: It's okay, hijo. You don't have to know. Not today. What's this?

CHAC-MOOL: A tattoo. It's Chac-Mool.

MEDEA: Ya lo veo. Why'd you do it?

CHAC-MOOL: I dunno, I thought it'd be cool.

MEDEA: Cool.

CHAC-MOOL: I was preparing myself. A tattoo couldn't hurt no more than getting pierced.

MEDEA: Tattoos last forever.

CHAC-MOOL: So do scars.

MEDEA: Déjame ver. *(She traces the tattoo with her finger.)* You know what that bowl is for . . . there on his belly?

CHAC-MOOL: For sacrificed hearts. Chac-Mool carries them to the gods.

MEDEA: He's the messenger. Entre este mundo y el otro lado.

CHAC-MOOL: And he's a warrior, right? Isn't that what you always told me?

MEDEA: Sí . . .

CHAC-MOOL: What, Mom?

MEDEA: He's a fallen warrior, hijo.

CHAC-MOOL: Well, why would you name me like that, for someone who didn't win?

MEDEA: Winning's not the point. Anyway, it was better than your other name.

CHAC-MOOL: Yeah, but—

MEDEA: But what?

CHAC-MOOL: You never told me that part before is all.

[MAMA SAL enters.]

MAMA SAL: Por fin. Somebody's putting a damn hoe in the dirt out here. *(She bends down to finger the earth.)* It's more sand than anything else.

CHAC-MOOL: The corn's gonna be blue, Bisabuela.

MAMA SAL: Blue maíz.

CHAC-MOOL: It's an experiment. Everybody says it grows best in Aztlán, but Luna says —

MAMA SAL: Blue corn. Bueno, just don't start putting huevos on top of your enchiladas like they do en Nuevo México.

CHAC-MOOL: Ugh.

MEDEA: That's how they eat 'em in Aztlán.

MAMA SAL: Ni modo. If you can grow corn and you know how to light a fire, you'll never be hungry, Chac-Mool. Never.

[The sudden blast of salsa music from a small radio. Lots of static. THE PRISON GUARD enters, announces:]

PRISON GUARD: The Hungry Woman.

[S/he grabs MEDEA's hand to escort her over to the hospital. MEDEA hesitates, looks to her son. CHAC-MOOL and MAMA SAL exit.]

Scene Five

[After depositing MEDEA in her hospital room, GUARD joins NURSE in their on-going dominoes game. MEDEA sits and begins pumping her

breasts, one at a time. She puts her index finger below the breast and places her thumb above, her fingers rolling down to meet at the nipple. MEDEA looks for milk at the tip of her nipple, touches it lightly, brings the faint yellow liquid from her fingertips to her lips.]

MEDEA: It was true what Jasón claimed, that I was unfaithful to him. True, I was in the midst of an insatiable love affair. No, it *did* satiate. Did it begin when my son first put his spoon-sized mouth to my breast? Yes, there our union was consummated, there in the circle of his ruby mouth. A ring of pure animal need taking hold of me. It was a secret Jasón named, stripped to expose us—mother and child— naked and clinging primordial to each other.

[JASÓN appears, in memory, isolated in his own light. He paces nervously.]

JASÓN: I want a wife, Medea. It's not natural!

MEDEA: Each night I could hear Jasón circling outside our bedroom window, over and over again, pissing out the boundaries of what he knew he could never enter. Only protect. Defend. Mark as his domain. *(Suddenly)* Nurse! Nurse! They're spilling again. ¡Ay diosa! ¡Apúrate, vieja!

[NURSE tosses a box of nursing pads onto the bed. Lights fade on JASÓN.]

NURSE: If you'd leave your pezones alone, you wouldn't be needing these.

[MEDEA opens up the box, stuffs a pad in each cup of her bra.]

MEDEA: I never really weaned my son. One day, he just stopped wanting it. It was peer pressure. He was three years old. I call him over to me. "Mijito," I say, "¿quieres chichi?" He is on his way out to play. I remember his playmate, that little Rudy boy at the doorway. And I show Chac-Mool my breast. His eyes pass over me. Lizard eyes. Cold. "Not now, Mom," he says. Like a man. I knew then that he already wanted to be away from me, to grow up to suck on some other woman's milk-less tit.

NURSE: Took it personally, did you?

MEDEA: There's nothing more personal than the love between a mother and child. You wouldn't know. You are childless, a dull mule who can't reproduce. I will always be more woman than you.

NURSE: I was sterilized. Puerto Rico. 1965.

MEDEA: *(Suddenly)* Boriquén is not free! Puerto Rico does not remember your name. Boriquén forgets her faithful daughter.

NURSE: No me insultes con tus palabras.

MEDEA: No te insulto. Te honro. *(Slumping back onto the bed)* Ay! I'm getting as old and as stupid as you.

NURSE: I'm stupid!? You're talking about me?

MEDEA: ¿Qué crees? You see somebody else in this room right now besides us loony tunes y ese maricón p'alla? *(The Guard glares back at her.)*

NURSE: I'm not the lunatic. I can leave here. 3 pm every day. It's a job.

MEDEA: Then get to work and change the goddamn station. I'm sick of that salsa shit!

[GUARD turns up volume. It's pure static now.]

MEDEA: *(To GUARD)* Cabrona!

NURSE: ¡Ya basta! ¡Apágala! *(GUARD turns off the radio.)* Y no le haces caso. You seen her girlfriend? ¡B-u-u-u-cha!

[Sound of phone ringing, ringing, ringing. MEDEA rushes to the mirror excitedly, finger-combs her hair, composes herself, then speaks into the mirror as if on a telephone. JASÓN again appears in memory.]

MEDEA: There's no need for name-calling, Jasón.

JASÓN: I did return your call.

MEDEA: Yes, thank you.

JASÓN: Well, what is it?

MEDEA: I was wondering about my status.

JASÓN: Your status? I thought this was about the boy.

MEDEA: You will abandon his mother again?

JASÓN: I didn't—

MEDEA: Technically I still hold the right to return. My land—

JASÓN: Is in my custody.

MEDEA: Yes.

JASÓN: You want to come back then.

MEDEA: I want to know my status.

JASÓN: That's simple. Give up the dyke. Nothing's changed.

MEDEA: Her name is Luna, Jasón.

JASÓN: Yes, Luna. How could I forget?

MEDEA: And your marriage?

JASÓN: My marriage is another matter.

MEDEA: It matters to me.

JASÓN: It does . . . ?

MEDEA: . . . Yes.

> [*Lights fade on JASÓN as the phone begins to ring again. MEDEA holds her ears against the sound.*]

Scene Six

> [*The ringing is drowned out by the sounds of a tenement basement: clanking old water pipes, the exhausted rotation of aging industrial-*]

sized washing machines, the dripping fan of an air conditioner circa 1970.]

PRISON GUARD: *(Announcing from her dominoes table)* A weekday evening in Phoenix. One year ago, again.

[S/he turns back to the game. Lights crossfade to LUNA in the basement laundry room of the apartment building. She and SAVANNAH fold clothes.]

LUNA: I come down here just to get away from Medea sometimes. I sit up on top of the dryer and my thighs stay warm in winter. In the summer, it's cooler here in the darkness.

SAVANNAH: Yeah, a regular paradise down here.

LUNA: I feel like I can breathe better. I got all my sculpting stuff down here, locked up in that cupboard. I'm just waiting to save up for enough clay to put my hands onto something. The rest of the stuff in there is mostly household tools. Sometimes I open it just to see all the glass jars of nails and screws all lined up on the shelves and my hand drill and wrenches all hanging real neat. She never comes in to mess things up. She never knows where a hammer is or a Phillips. She doesn't need to. She lives on beauty alone.

SAVANNAH: Rent still gotta get paid by somebody.

LUNA: Upstairs it's pure chaos. It's like I can't stop moving, working, cleaning. I hear my voice and it's my mother's voice, nagging. I'm nagging like a frustrated housewife. I bitch. I bitch about the laundry that I never stop doing, the dishes that never stop piling piling up, the newspapers . . . news from the rest of the world, always a dozen days old, recycled magazines, 4th-class mailers never opened. All she does is read and discard, read and discard right where she finished the last line of print. The couch, the toilet, the kitchen table, the bed. Her shoes and stockings and bra come off right there, too. She says she doesn't give a damn if I feel exploited. She says who asked you to be a housewife? "¿Quién te manda? I want a lover, not a vieja." I think what she really wants is a man. I hear her on the phone negotiating with that self-conscious lilt in her voice. I didn't even like it when she used to "lilt" me.

SAVANNAH: Who she talking to?

LUNA: I don't know. Friends. Enemies. She says it's for Chac. That's all she says.

SAVANNAH: Luna, stop waiting on her.

LUNA: I can't. I feel like I can't breathe like all the shit in the house, the plates with the stuck-on egg, the chorizo grease in the skillet, the spilled powder milk and crumbs on the floor, the unmade bed, the towels on the floor of every room in the house . . . that all of it is conspiring against me, suckin' up all the air in that apartment.

SAVANNAH: You trippin' bad.

LUNA: Maybe I am. *(Putting a clean tee shirt to her face, breathing in)* No smell sweeter.

SAVANNAH: What's that?

LUNA: Liquid Tide.

SAVANNAH: Imported?

LUNA: Terrible for the environment, but who gives a shit about the environment here.

SAVANNAH: Nobody I know.

LUNA: It's such a clean smell. The cotton. I put my nose inside here and everything is organized. Everything is sweet and well-placed.

[MEDEA enters. SAVANNAH spies her first.]

SAVANNAH: Don't look now, here comes Beauty's Beast.

MEDEA: Sniffing clothes again?

LUNA: Do you want something, Medea?

MEDEA: Oh, am I interrupting?

SAVANNAH: No, I was just leaving.

MEDEA: Not on my account, I hope.

SAVANNAH: See you tonight, Luna.

LUNA: See ya. *(SAVANNAH exits.)*

MEDEA: What was that all about?

LUNA: What do you want, Medea?

MEDEA: Why are you hiding from me?

LUNA: I'm not hiding from you.

MEDEA: No? Then what's this?

[MEDEA stretches out a long strand of hair in front of LUNA's face.]

LUNA: What? It's hair.

MEDEA: It's not my hair.

LUNA: Okay . . . so?

MEDEA: It's not yours . . . too coarse. Whose is it? I found it in our bed.

LUNA: I don't know whose hair it is.

MEDEA: Are you having an affair?

LUNA: That's too easy, Medea! You can't get rid of me that easy.

MEDEA: Answer me.

LUNA: Look, there are forty-five apartments in this project, Medea, housing every kind of queen and queer and party animal in Phoenix. I don't know who puts their clothes in the dryer ahead of me and got their pelito stuck onto our sábanas.

MEDEA: Take the whine out of your voice.

LUNA: I'm not whining.

MEDEA: You're weak. You don't love me. You just follow rules. You're afraid of me. Do you think that makes me feel safe?

LUNA: No, I imagine it doesn't.

[She gathers up the clothes basket.]

MEDEA: *(Grabbing LUNA)* Don't you give up on me. ¿M'oyes?

LUNA: *(Breaking her hold)* I'm getting out of here.

MEDEA: Where to? To see one of your "girlfriends?"

LUNA: Yes, to tell you the truth I miss them a lot right now. Just thought I'd drink a coupla beers with some plain ole unequivocal tortilleras.

MEDEA: Fight for me, cabrona. You're worse than a man.

LUNA: You oughta know.

[LUNA drops the clothes basket and exits into the garden where MAMA SAL and CHAC-MOOL sit surrounded by the noises of the city and a heavy evening smog. A mournful animal cry is heard. They all stop for a moment at the sound. CHAC-MOOL and MAMA SAL wait for LUNA to say something. She looks at them, then exits without a word. The cry is heard again.]

MAMA SAL: Gives you chicken skin, doesn't it?

CHAC-MOOL: Sounds like a baby crying.

MAMA SAL: They moan like that when they're lonely for their machos. *(Pause)* I had a cat like that once. She was wanting it so bad, she clawed a hole through the screen door to get out. In no time, I had a small mountain of gatitos in my closet. Están locas when they're in heat. *[The cry sounds again.]*

MAMA SAL: She got such a lonesome llanto. Es el llanto de La Llorona.

CHAC-MOOL: La Llorona never scared me.

MAMA SAL: No? Not even when you was a little esquincle?

CHAC-MOOL: No, I felt sorry for her, not scared.

MAMA SAL: Pues a mí, me asustaba mucho ella.

CHAC-MOOL: I remember hearing her out there in the cañon when I was real little, right before we left Aztlán. The wind would kick up 'bout the same time every night. Her voice was inside the wind. I'd hear my Mom get up, go check the windows and doors, then go back to sleep. It sounded like the whole canyon was cryin'. *(Pause)* I felt like she was telling me her side of the story, like I was the only one that heard it like that.

MAMA SAL: Maybe you were.

[CHAC-MOOL *watches the sky. The sounds of the city in the distance: sirens, screeching cars, low-flying police helicopters.*]

CHAC-MOOL: They're fighting all the time now, you know, my mom and Luna.

MAMA SAL: Yo sé. A veces puede ser muy sangrona tu mamá.

CHAC-MOOL: What?

MAMA SAL: Don't make a mother choose between blood and love.

Scene Seven

[*The local bar.* "Crazy" *plays on the juke box. SAVANNAH and TATTOO ARTIST are dancing a slow number. LUNA watches the dance floor, nursing a beer.*]

LUNA: Turn off that white-girl shit!

[SAVANNAH *crosses to LUNA.*]

SAVANNAH: Let's go now, Luna. It's almost closing.

LUNA: Shit, in Aztlán the night would barely be starting right now. In Tamoachán everything closes up tight as a virgin's thighs.

SAVANNAH: You're drunk.

LUNA: I'm not drunk. I'm bitter.

SAVANNAH: You're talking like a drunk.

LUNA: And you're just an old lesbian prude like the rest of our generation. All that twelve-stepping and disease in the 90s turned us into a buncha deadbeats. Let's go to la taquería, I need to soak up the tequila.

SAVANNAH: Nothing's open now.

LUNA: The taquería is.

SAVANNAH: Which taquería?

LUNA: The one that leaves all the jalapeños out on the table. St. Josie's or whatever its name is. You know how they have those sweet little plastic bowls in pink and yellow and turquoise on the table filled with jalapeños floating around with slices of carrots. Shit, the carrots are as hot as the chiles after floating around so long in the same juices.

SAVANNAH: You see you got to be careful who you float around with. You ready?

LUNA: Wait. I have to go to the head. *(She crosses to a bathroom stall.)* Hold the door will you, baby? The lock's busted. *(SAVANNAH does.)* This place is such a dive. You ever known a nice lesbian bar? What did gay liberation ever do for colored dykes? We might as well be back all closeted-up like Mama Sal's stories of "the life" half-century ago, sharing the dance floor with drag queens and ho's, waiting for the cops to come in and bust our butts. This place is a dump.

SAVANNAH: You wanna talk about it, Luna?

LUNA: What? About what a dump this place is? Shit. No toilet paper. Pass me a paper towel, baby.

SAVANNAH: *(Checking the dispenser)* There isn't any.

LUNA: I hate drip drying. You got anything?

SAVANNAH: *(Takes a Kleenex from her bag, passes it to her.)* Girl, here.

LUNA Thanks. I *am* talking about it, talking about all the things Medea says every time I try to bring her to a joint like this.

[*LUNA comes out of the stall. SAVANNAH half-blocks the door with her body.*]

LUNA: What? What is it, Savannah?

SAVANNAH: Luna, I'm tired.

LUNA: Well, let's go —

SAVANNAH: I'm tired of seeing someone I love being played. Medea wants out, Luna. The writing's on the fuckin' bathroom wall.

LUNA: ¿Y. . . qué?

SAVANNAH: And I want . . . in.

LUNA: Ah, Savannah. Don't tell me that.

SAVANNAH: How long have you known me?

LUNA: I don't know. A long time.

SAVANNAH: Five years.

LUNA: Okay.

SAVANNAH: I'm here when you want it.

LUNA: "It." Like that?

SAVANNAH: Like that.

LUNA: But you're my buddy.

SAVANNAH: Fuck your "buddy."

LUNA: I don't wannu!

[They both bust up. SAVANNAH pins LUNA up against the wall.]

LUNA: Savannah, I —

[SAVANNAH kisses her deeply.]

LUNA: She's always been jealous of you.

SAVANNAH: I know. She ain't all crazy.

LUNA: C'mon. I gotta get home.

[They wrap their arms around each other's shoulders and sing "Crazy" as they exit.]

Scene Eight

[MEDEA lies on top of her bed still dressed after a night drinking alone.]

MEDEA: You once thought me beautiful, Lunita. My hair the silky dark-ness of a raven's, the cruelty of Edgar Allen Poe's own, I know. I know you think me cruel. But you must like it, in a way, the cry of the dead seeping through floorboards, all my angry ancestors incensed by something you haven't figured out yet: your seamless face, the natural blush on your peach-down cheeks, a mamá who loved you, if only too much.

[LUNA enters, quietly removes her shoes, then realizes Medea is still awake.]

LUNA: Medea.

MEDEA : Oh, good. It's you.

LUNA: Medea, why are you still up?

MEDEA Take my body, baby.

LUNA: Were you waiting up for me?

MEDEA: I don't want to watch it descend into the earth.

LUNA: C'mon, let me get you into the bed.

[*LUNA stumbles across an empty fifth of tequila.*]

LUNA: Shit.

MEDEA: Gravity, fucking gravity.

LUNA: How much did you drink?

MEDEA: The earth has become my enemy.

LUNA: I'm gonna get you some aspirins. (*MEDEA stops her.*)

MEDEA: I don't even remember being nineteen. Where you been, amor? You shouldn't leave me alone so much.

LUNA: You never want to come with me.

MEDEA: I don't like being alone. It's not . . . safe. I don't trust myself.

LUNA: Let's get your clothes off.

[*LUNA starts to undress MEDEA.*]

MEDEA: I used to have spectacular thighs. Remember, Lunita?

LUNA: You still do.

MEDEA: Remember how I'd wrap my thighs around your boy's face. (*Holding her face*) How come I called it a boy's face when you're so female?

LUNA: (*Pulling away*) Just macha, Medea.

MEDEA: A boy's hunger, that's what I saw there in those dark eyes resting between my legs. Luna, why would you look at me that way?

LUNA: What way, amor?

MEDEA: Like you didn't have what I had, like you didn't have nalgas, senos mas firmes que yo, a pussy . . . that perfect triangle of black hair . . .

LUNA: I'm just a jota, baby.

MEDEA: That's a stupid response.

LUNA: Don't be cruel.

MEDEA: I'm not cruel, I'm dying. Dying to make sense of it. How does it start? How does it vanish? How is it you used to drink from me as if you yourself didn't taste the same coppered richness when you brought your own bloody fingers to your mouth. As if when you drew a woman's shape with your sculptor's hands, you didn't find the same diosa curves and valleys when you bathed yourself each day. Eres mujer. But for you, falling in love is to think nothing of yourself, your own body. In the beginning all was me.

LUNA: Yes, in the beginning.

MEDEA: And now?

LUNA: It's different now. You get used to each other. It's . . . normal.

MEDEA: I loathe normal. At night, I would lay awake and wonder, how is it she could worship me so and not be banished? But then you were already banished. And now, that's the road I walk, too.

LUNA: Medea, that was seven years ago.

MEDEA: I had always imagined we'd return to Aztlán one day with my son grown. I thought they'd change their mind, say it was all a mistake.

LUNA: Medea, did you talk to Jasón tonight?

MEDEA: Yes.

LUNA: What does he want?

MEDEA: Chac-Mool.

LUNA: When?

MEDEA: Now. Tomorrow. No sé. Soon. He's sending custody papers. She's barren.

LUNA: What?

MEDEA: The virgin bride. Está vacía.

LUNA: He's still going to marry her? *(MEDEA nods.)* Damn, he must love her.

MEDEA: She can still fuck, Luna.

LUNA: I'm . . . sorry.

[MEDEA starts to get up.]

LUNA: Don't. C'mere . . . Medea.

MEDEA: He wants my boy.

LUNA: I know.

MEDEA: I know Jasón, he won't stop 'til he has him.

LUNA: Medea, come back to bed. Please.

[MEDEA goes to her. LUNA brings MEDEA into the bed, holds her. Lighting transition. LUNA makes love to MEDEA with her mouth.]

LUNA: Creation Myth. In the place where the spirits live, there was once a woman who cried constantly for food. She had mouths everywhere. In her wrists, elbows, ankles, knees. . . . And every mouth was hungry y bien gritona. To comfort la pobre, the spirits flew down and began to make grass and flowers from the dirt-brown of her skin. From her greñas, they made forests. From those ojos negros, pools and springs. And from the slopes of her shoulders and senos, they made mountains y valles. At last she will be satisfied, they thought. Pero, just like before, her mouths were everywhere, biting and moaning . . . opening and snapping shut. They would never be filled. *(Pause)* Sometimes por la noche, when the wind blows, you can hear her crying for food. *

[After sex]

LUNA: Tell me who you were with him.

MEDEA: It still interests you?

LUNA: Yes.

MEDEA: Why?

LUNA: It gives me something . . . somehow.

MEDEA: What?

LUNA: I don't know. That I have you that way, like he did. But different. Knowing he wasn't—

MEDEA: . . . Enough?

LUNA: Yes.

MEDEA: You haven't changed.

[They kiss again.]

LUNA: Some days I think I have been with you forever. Seven years . . . forever. Chac-Mool is our measuring stick, like the pencil scratches on the kitchen wall, marking out our time together. When that last mark passed the height of my own head, I thought . . . "where do we go from here?" No growing left to do. I can hardly remember being with other women.

MEDEA: I remember. You being with other women.

*From *The Hungry Woman: Myths and Legends of the Aztecs*. John Bierhorst, ed. New York: William Morrow & Co, 1984.

LUNA: So, do we just go back to where we started? Do we return to zero?

MEDEA: Zero. A good place to be. I wish I had the guts.

LUNA: *(Tries to bring MEDEA into her arms again, MEDEA resists.)*
Medea.

MEDEA: It doesn't matter now. I am the last one to make this journey.
My tragedy will be an example to all women like me. Vain women
who only know to be the beloved. Such an example I shall be that
no woman will dare to transgress those boundaries again. You,
you and your kind, have no choice. You were born to be a lover
of women, to grow hands that could transform a woman like those
blocks of faceless stone you turn into diosas. I, my kind, am a dying
breed of female. I am the last one to make this crossing, the border
has closed behind me. There will be no more room for transgressions.

Scene Nine

[MEDEA rises from the bed, slips on a black dress. LUNA observes.]

MEDEA: Help me. *(Indicating her zipper)*

*[LUNA doesn't. The PRISON GUARD enters, zips up MEDEA's
dress and hands LUNA a small stack of letters.]*

PRISON GUARD: A few months later. It is stifling hot in exile. *(S/he exits.)*

LUNA: Where are you going? . . . To him?

MEDEA: Yes.

[MEDEA arranges her face in the mirror.]

LUNA: Why are you courting his illusions, Medea?

MEDEA: What illusions?

LUNA: That you're not a lesbian.

MEDEA: I'm not?

LUNA: You know lesbianism is a lot like virginity, you can't recycle it. You don't get to say oops, sorry, I changed my mind, I didn't mean those seven years in her bed.

MEDEA: What do you want me to do, shove it in his face?

LUNA: Yeah. I want you to shove it in his face. I want you to tell him, "¿Recuerdas, Jasón? The mother of your son is a dyke. She licks panocha and loves it."

MEDEA: So, he can take my son away for good.

LUNA: Oh, he doesn't just want the "Warrior-son," he wants it all: "Virgin-bride," "Aztec-goddess. . . ." Or can't you read between the lines?

[She throws the letters to her. They fall on the floor between them.]

MEDEA: Where did you find them?

LUNA: Where you left them.

MEDEA: You rummaged.

LUNA: Not much.

MEDEA: I'll keep my son any way I have to.

LUNA: That's what I'm afraid of.

MEDEA: ¿No ves? You've seen the letters. I still have allies there. People don't forget so easy. I'm building a bridge back. For both of us. I'll send for you.

LUNA: I don't think so, Medea. I'm not the revolutionary they have in mind.

MEDEA: Luna.

LUNA: I don't know what's going on with you. It's like the thought of losing Chac . . . no kid between us . . . and we got nothing to disguise what we are to each other. Maybe for you, Chac-Mool somehow makes us less lesbian.

MEDEA: Maybe.

LUNA: Well, it's too late, Medea. You can't go back there. I know your
secrets. Your secrets have been safe with me. All of them, like sacred
relics, carefully guarded. I watch them spill out of you in our love-
making and I tell no one. I don't even tell you what I can testify to
in every sheet you drench with your desire. Let me remind you of
the first time. The magic. The disappearing act. My hands vanishing
inside you. Your grito. "Where are your hands?" you cry. They move
inside of you and you thank me with your eyes. For this, I forgive
you everything. And we start another day. You've changed, Medea. You
don't know it yet, but you won't ever be able to go back to Aztlán or to
any man. You've been ruined by me. My hands have ruined you.

[There is a pause. MEDEA picks up the letters.]

MEDEA: I'm not you, Luna. I wasn't born that way, the way you like to
brag. I'm just a woman worried about keeping her son. You act so
damn free. You're not free.

LUNA: No, I live in the fuckin' colony of my so-called liberators.

MEDEA: You don't even know your own prison. I'm right in your face
everyday. We sleep together, eat together, raise my child together, and
some half-man writes me a few lies and you give it all your attention.
I'm not even in the equation, except as the premio at the end of your
contest with him. You can't beat Jasón, Luna. Isn't this queer ghetto
proof of that?

LUNA: Tell yourself that. I don't want to beat him.

MEDEA: No?

LUNA: No.

MEDEA: You're lying. First to yourself, then to me. When you stopped
wanting to beat him, you stopped wanting me.

LUNA: That's not true.

MEDEA: Now he's back in our lives and you're on top of me again like a
teenage boy.

LUNA: Are you complaining?

MEDEA: Yes. I want to be left alone.

LUNA: . . . With your thoughts?

MEDEA: Yes.

LUNA: They betray me.

MEDEA: They betray my unhappiness.

LUNA: With me.

MEDEA: With all of this . . . failure.

LUNA: You hate it here that much.

MEDEA: That much. But I promise you, I hate my countrymen even more.

LUNA: He can hurt us, Medea.

MEDEA: Yo sé.

LUNA: He's already hurting us. You don't flirt with power. You fight it.

> [LUNA *exits and crosses out the front of the building where MAMA* SAL *sits smoking her pipe. Upstage MEDEA continues dressing: nylons, make-up, heels, etc.*]

MAMA SAL: In a hurry?

LUNA: I . . . no. You got a cigarette?

MAMA SAL: *(Feigned innocence)* Moi?

LUNA: Give me a cigarette, Mama Sal.

> [*She does.* LUNA *lights up.*]

MAMA SAL: ¿Pa' dónde ibas?

LUNA: I dunno. Out. Away.

[LUNA paces. Smokes.]

MAMA SAL: When you're a girl, hija, and a Mexican, you learn purty quick that you got only one shot at being a woman and that's being a mother.

LUNA: Tell Medea. She's the mother, not me.

MAMA SAL: You go from a daughter to mother, and there's nothing in-between. That's the law of our people written como los diez commandments on the metate stone from the beginning of all time.

LUNA: Well, that ain't my story.

MAMA SAL: Exacto. You go and change the law. You leave your mother and go out and live on your own.

LUNA: That's right.

MAMA SAL: You learn how to tear down walls and put them up again. Hasta tu propia casa, you build with your own hands. Still, you can't forget your mother, even when you try to.

LUNA: Sal, I—

MAMA SAL: You search for a woman. You find many womans. But still you feel your daughter-hands are sleeping. You meet Medea—

LUNA: Medea.

MAMA SAL: And your whole body wakes up to the empty places inside her. You twist and deform yourself to fill her. You turn out crooked. *(Pause)* Leave her, Luna. She's not the woman for you.

LUNA: She's your granddaughter.

MAMA SAL: Leave her, te digo. I say that out of love for you both.

[LUNA tosses the cigarette to the ground and exits.]

Scene Ten

> [*MEDEA, in black silk dress, stands before the altar of Coatlicue. She burns copal.*]

MEDEA:
> Madre, Coatlicue.
> I want to know your sweet fury.
> Teach me your seductive magic,
> your beauty and rage.
> Make Jasón small and weak.
> Make him shiver
> within the folds of my serpent skin.
>
> He feared me before.
> Help me make him remember why.

> [*Lighting transition. JASÓN appears. He stares out a window. Moonlight bathes his face.*]

JASÓN: There was a time when I remembered being no one or as close to no one as possible. As no one as any Mexican man on that midnight train passing through Puebla. A full moon. A lonesomeness so full, so complete.

> [*MEDEA crosses to him.*]

MEDEA: Te da tanta nostalgia being with me?

JASÓN: A little, I guess. I'm glad to see you face-to-face. The letters . . . your words are very persuasive.

MEDEA: I was a writer once, too, remember?

JASÓN: Of course.

> [*Jasón crosses to a table, unwraps the plastic off a glass.*]

JASÓN: Drink?

MEDEA: Yes, thank you.

JASÓN: Sorry, the glassware's not too fancy.

MEDEA: Border motels.

JASÓN: Yeah, I'm sorry. I didn't know where else to meet. Somewhere out of the public eye.

MEDEA: I'm a big girl, Jasón. I can take care of myself.

JASÓN: Obviously. Still, you certainly dressed for the occasion.

MEDEA: It bothers you?

JASÓN: No, I wouldn't say "bother." "Torment" is the word I'd use.

[*She laughs.*]

JASÓN: *(Enjoying it)* Are you trying to torment me, Medea?

MEDEA: Don't flatter yourself, Jasón. I wore this dress for myself. That's something few of my lovers have ever understood. The clothes are for me. The feel of silk against my thigh, the caress of a satin slip over my breasts, the scent of musk when I bury my own face into the pillow of my arm.

JASÓN: You should live on an island.

MEDEA: No, occasionally I need someone to accuse me of tormenting them with my beauty. Do you find me beautiful, Jasón?

JASÓN: You know I do.

MEDEA: Still?

JASÓN: Yes. Very.

[*She looks hard at him for a moment.*]

MEDEA: You're kind. Nos 'stamos poniendo viejos ¿no, Jasón?

JASÓN: No tanto. You look fine . . . good for your age.

MEDEA: Yes. My age. My eyelids—

JASÓN: You've got beautiful eyes. I always told you that.

MEDEA: Obsidian jewels you called them.

JASÓN: I did.

MEDEA: It's different for a man. They're young at fifty. Sixty, even. Look at you, marrying a woman a third of your age.

JASÓN: I guess I—

MEDEA: I'm jealous of her, Jasón. Your new young love.

JASÓN: You're jealous?

MEDEA: My vanity is no secret. In an odd way, I grew to kind of rely on your devotion, safely distanced as it was. I derived comfort out of knowing that, even in my exile, you thought of me. You did think of me, didn't you?

JASÓN: At one time . . . daily.

MEDEA: No longer?

JASÓN: One doesn't stop thinking of you, Medea. The thoughts merely grow less . . . insistent.

[MEDEA smiles. JASÓN takes hold of her hand.]

JASÓN: Medea, why the sudden change of heart?

MEDEA: I want what's best for my son. He'll be forgotten here in this ghetto.

JASÓN: I'm . . . sorry.

MEDEA: Are you?

JASÓN: You don't have to stay here either, you know.

MEDEA: I don't know that.

JASÓN: You're not a lesbian, Medea, for chrissake. This is a masquerade.

MEDEA: A seven-year-old one?

JASÓN: I'm not saying that you have no feelings for the relationship, but . . . you're not a Luna.

MEDEA: *(Sadly)* No, I'm not.

JASÓN: I want you to reconsider.

[*There is a pause.*]

MEDEA: After the War . . . before Chac-Mool, I felt completely naked in the world. No child to clothe me in his thoughtless need, to clothe the invading lack of purpose in my life. I can't go back to that.

JASÓN: You don't have to.

MEDEA: Then I wasn't mistaken?

JASÓN: No.

[*He takes her into his arms. They kiss and begin to make love.*]

Act II

Prelude

[Pre-Columbian Meso-American music. In the semi-darkness, the stone image of Coatlicue becomes illuminated. The CIHUATATEO stand sentinel beside it.]

CIHUATATEO EAST: This is how all nights begin and end.

*[MEDEA emerges from the icon as the "living COATLICUE."
She is uncombed and wears only a black slip. CIHUATATEO
EAST wraps an apron around MEDEA's waist and CIHUATATEO
NORTH hands her a broom. MEDEA begins sweeping.]*

CIHUATATEO EAST: A long time ago, before the Aztec war of the flowers, before war, Coatlicue, la mera madre diosa, was sweeping on top of the mountain, Coatepec, when she encounters two delicate plumitas. She stuffs the feathers into her apron, thinking later she might weave them into a cloth for her altar. But suddenly, secretly, the feathers begin to gestate there by her womb, y de repente, Coatlicue, goddess of Creation and Destruction, becomes pregnant.

Now, Coatlicue es una anciana, bien beyond the age of fertility, so when her daughter, Coyolxauhqui, learns of the boy-to-be-born, traición is what she smells entre los cuatros vientos.

[LUNA appears as COYOLXAUHQUI.]

COYOLXAUHQUI: You betrayed me, Madre.

CIHUATATEO EAST: So, along with her 'manitos, "The Four Hundred Stars," Coyolxauhqui conspires to kill the Mother-god.

CIHUATATEO CORO:
>The light of the son
>will eclipse your daughter's glow
>hold you under fire
>in the heat of his embrace

[The birth of the Aztec sun-god, Huitzilopotchli, is enacted. CHAC-MOOL as the sun-god emerges, in full Aztec regalia, from the icon/woman, COATLICUE.]

CIHUATATEO EAST: Pero, Huitzilopotchli, that's him, el diosito inside Coatlicue, he ain't gonna punk out on his mami. A hummingbird buzzes by and gives the little sun-god the 4-1-1 about the planned matricide, and the vatito is quick to respond.

HUITZILOPOTCHI: Cuenta conmigo, jefa. I got it all under control.

[Brother and sister, HUITZILOPOTCHLI and COYOLXAUQUI, as the gods of day and night, battle for dominion over the heavens.]

CIHUATATEO EAST: With filero flying, Huitzilopotchli chops off his sister's head.

HUITZILOPOTCHLI: Sas!

CIHUATATEO CORO:
>Y sus senos
>las manos
>las piernas
>los dedos

[COYOLXAUHQUI is dismembered.]

HUITZILOPOTCHLI: Is this my sister's moonface I hold bleeding between my hands? I exile you foreign and female into that vast hole of darkness that is your home. — getting exiled because lesbian?

[He tosses "the head" into the heavens. They all watch the moon rise into the night sky.]

COATLICUE: La Luna!

CIHUATATEO EAST: This is how all nights begin and end.

Scene One

> *[The psychiatric ward. The PRISON GUARD stacks dominoes in the corner. MEDEA stands at the barred window. The shadow of the bars from the moon's reflection crosses her face. NURSE observes her.]*

NURSE: The moon was beautiful out tonight, did you see it?

MEDEA: No Luna. Ya no Luna.

NURSE: Whadya say, honey?

> *[MEDEA does not respond. She cranes her neck to feel more of the moon on her face.]*

NURSE: *(To Guard)* Bendita. She's been walking around in a funk all day. The girlfriend didn't come.

MEDEA: No Luna.

It was a moonless night. Black sky. There had to be stars, but I don't remember any. All four hundred vanished into thin mountain air. And the brother-god was born back into our family, returned a warrior decorated. I remember the decoration, the medal leaving an imprint in my cheek when he brought me to his chest and squeezed. He taught me how to squeeze, not too hard, just the right amount of pressure, the right curve in my little girl's palm.

At first, when he opened his zipper, it was like "Let's make a deal!" "What's behind the curtain?" And what was behind the curtain was grown-up and a mystery machine, the way it could inflate and deflate just by thinking he told me, he could think it hard and tried to teach me hard thoughts, too. And Mami said . . .

> *[Lighting transition. NURSE becomes MEDEA's mother in memory. Their lines overlap one another at each slash.]*

illustration
1

NURSE: Wait on your brother. Give your brother whatever he wants.

MEDEA: Shoes shined, shirts ironed, money from your torito piggy bank/ for putas and pisto.

NURSE: Give him whatever he/ needs.

MEDEA: Cuz he's the only man in the/ family.

NURSE: Your father isn't worth two cents,/ not mean enough.

MEDEA: Just a llorón who don't know how to cheat a little/ to make a little extra.

NURSE: Be good to your brother, give him/ whatever he wants.

MEDEA: Cuz God has been good to us bringing him home in one piece/ and not crazy.

NURSE: When the rest of the barrio boys are coming home in burlap bags.

MEDEA: And stiff canvas flags folded into triangles.

[*MEDEA lets out a deep wail. NURSE goes to her.*]

MEDEA: Saturday is almost over and she didn't come, Nurse.

NURSE: She musta been otherwise occupied.

[*PRISON GUARD announces.*]

PRISON GUARD: "Otherwise occupied." Luna is arrested at the border.

[*NURSE escorts MEDEA offstage. GUARD crosses to LUNA, who appears in a kind of sack dress, bare legs and feet. S/he ties LUNA's hands behind her back with the black bandanna, sits LUNA down in the "interrogation room." A huge spotlight glares into LUNA's face.*]

BORDER GUARD: Why did you cross the border?

LUNA: I was on my way to her.

BORDER GUARD: To whom?

LUNA: I got distracted.

BORDER GUARD: Whom were you to meet?

LUNA: No one. I was visiting the sick. It was a Saturday.

BORDER GUARD: Today is Monday.

LUNA: There was a song on the bus. It was her song. *(Half-singing)*

"Soy como el viento que corre
alrededor d'este mundo . . . "

BORDER GUARD: But you hadn't a work permit.

LUNA: I was denied one.

BORDER GUARD: You knew it was illegal.

LUNA: Yes.

BORDER GUARD: Then—

LUNA: I longed for Aztlán.

BORDER GUARD: Why did you break into the museum?

LUNA: I wanted to free them.

BORDER GUARD: Who?

LUNA: Those little female figures. Those tiny breasts and thick thighs, those ombligos y panzas de barro.

BORDER GUARD: Who were they to you, these figurines?

LUNA: Ancient little diosas, the size of children's toys. They were trapped, sir, behind the museum glass. They belonged to us. I remember them from my youth, going to visit them in my Catholic school uniform. I wanted to free my little sisters, trapped by history. I broke the glass.

BORDER GUARD: You stole them?

LUNA: No, m'am, I wanted only to hold them in my hands and feel what they had to teach me about their maker.

BORDER GUARD: And . . . ?

LUNA: We were not as we are now. We were not always fallen from the mountain.

BORDER GUARD: *(Announcing)* "Before the Fall. Mexican Pussy."

[*BORDER GUARD unties the "handcuffs" and hands LUNA a mirror.*]

BORDER GUARD: Ten, take a look.

[*Música. Amalia Mendoza. LUNA brings the mirror up between her legs, studies herself. MEDEA enters, then hides as if in a game.*]

MEDEA: *(Singing)*
"Háblanme montes y valles
Grítanme piedras del campo . . ."

LUNA: *(Spying her)* Hey!

MEDEA: Don't stop.

LUNA: You busted me.

MEDEA: *(Very playful)* Nah, go on with what you were doing.

LUNA: I can't. Not with you watching me.

MEDEA: What were you doing?

LUNA: Seeing.

MEDEA: That's my mirror you're holding.

LUNA: I wanted to see through your reflection.

MEDEA: See what?

LUNA: What I got.

MEDEA: You don't know.

LUNA: No.

MEDEA: *(Going to her)* I can tell you what you got.

LUNA: I want to know for myself.

MEDEA: Well . . .

LUNA: Well, what?

MEDEA: What do you got?

LUNA: Hair. God, lots of hair all over the place. Unruly hair. Undisciplined hair. Pelo de rebeldía. *(MEDEA smiles, kneels at LUNA's feet.)* I have a Mexican pussy, did you know that? Definitely a Mexican pussy.

MEDEA: How's that?

LUNA: Mexican women always hide our private parts.

MEDEA: I'm Mexican.

LUNA: Yeah, but you're . . . different. Less hair.

MEDEA: Mas india.

LUNA: Prouder, more . . . available.

MEDEA: I don't know about that.

LUNA: I love your pussy.

MEDEA: I love your mouth.

> [MEDEA kisses her.]

LUNA: My private parts are a battleground. I see struggle there before I see beauty.

MEDEA: I see beauty.

LUNA: You have to dig for it. You have to be committed.

MEDEA: I'm committed.

LUNA: You weren't supposed to see me doing this.

[*MEDEA takes the mirror out of LUNA's hands, kisses her again, first on the mouth, then grabs LUNA by the hips, and goes down on her. LUNA holds MEDEA's hair like a rope between her fingers, she pulls her closer. THE BORDER GUARD enters.*]

BORDER GUARD: So, you confess to being a lesbian.

[*LUNA and MEDEA separate in a panic. The BORDER GUARD stands between them. MEDEA and LUNA hold each other's eyes from a distance.*]

LUNA: Can I be tried twice for the same crime?

THE BORDER GUARD: Answer the question. Do you desire—

LUNA: There was no passion there. By the end, it was a mindless reflex. The desire was gone from us months before or was it years? We fought about it. We slept as sisters. When she began to dream and the dream was bad, I just drew the curve of her back closer to me, placed her hands one on top of the other, and folded them into her belly with the unconsciousness of a sonámbula.

MEDEA: I am sleepwalking still. Even the smell of the sea has abandoned us.

[*Sudden police sirens and the spinning of blue and red police lights. MEDEA stands amid the circling colored lights. Trance-like, she cradles her arms as if holding an infant. LUNA approaches her.*]

MEDEA: Do you smell my baby's death?

LUNA: I can't.

MEDEA: Open the holes in your face and breathe. The breeze smells of sulfur. Do you smell it?

LUNA: I . . . don't know.

MEDEA: Where were you, Luna, when I needed you?

LUNA: In my cell, always in my nun's cell.

MEDEA: I hardly recognize you, wearing the skirt of a woman.

LUNA: I dressed to visit you. I visit you weekly. But you won't speak to me. Is it . . . *(the infant)* heavy?

MEDEA: A dead child weighs nothing in your arms. He is light as balsam wood, hollow inside. The spirit gives weight to the flesh. His spirit ya se fue.

LUNA: The child I carry is heavy.

MEDEA: Tienes que dar a luz.

[LUNA turns and exits, the CIHUATATEO enter.]

CIHUATATEO: *(Chanting)*
Allí viene La Llorona.
Rivers rising.
Cold-blooded babies at her breast.

[Wind rises, blends with the wailing of children. Then the cry of La Llorona, an ominous and chilling wail, fills the air.]

CIHUATATEO: A-y-y-y-y-y-y-y! MIS HIJOS! MIS HI-I-I-I-JOS!

[The CIHUATATEO dance as warrior women. They draw out maguey thorns, the size of hands, from their serpent's sashes. They pierce and slash themselves, wailing. They encircle MEDEA with the ghostly white veil of La Llorona. It is a river in the silver light. MEDEA and the sound of the children's cries drown beneath it. Black out.]

[LUNA is back in the "Interrogation Room." Many hours have transpired, she is clearly exhausted. She speaks almost deliriously. JASÓN appears in shadow behind THE BORDER GUARD.]

BORDER GUARD: Do you confess?

LUNA:
    I am
    awake
    to the sound
    of screaming
    her voice, too, she is
    screaming I
    can't remember when they merge
    Medea's voice
    with my own
    only opening my mouth
    swallowing
    air
    the cry coming out
    the man
    in the doorway, a shadow
    a stranger
    a lover
    a rapist
    I
    can't know
    for sure
    I
    inside time stop time
    what to do
    when he
    enters
    the room
    his size immense
    filling the doorway
    what to do
    when he
    steps
    one
    foot
    inside
    the room
    I . . .

BORDER GUARD: Stop it. Speak sensibly. You are talking in circles!

LUNA: *(She composes herself)* When Jasón . . . found us—

BORDER GUARD: Yes. Go on.

JASÓN: When I found them in bed together, I remember I just stood there, staring at them.

BORDER GUARD: And then?

LUNA: Then . . . nothing.

JASÓN: *(Simultaneously)* Nothing.

BORDER GUARD: Nothing?

LUNA: He had a very . . . sad look on his face . . . disappointed, kind of.

JASÓN: I just turned away and walked into my study. I was waiting for her, waiting for an explanation.

LUNA: She got up and left me in the bed. I could hear them down the hall.

JASÓN: We fought.

LUNA: In hushed voices. I slipped out without their noticing. What else was there to do? The next morning, she shows up with the kid on my doorstep. He was five years old. She didn't know where else to go, she told me. I was the reason for it. I was the lesbian.

JASÓN (LUNA): I (He) never even came looking for them (us).

BORDER GUARD: That's it?

LUNA: No. She was exiled.

JASÓN: Medea was never to return to Aztlán.

[Black out.]

Scene Two

> [*CHAC-MOOL enters angrily with a armful of blue corn and a cooking pot. He goes to the kitchen table and begins stripping the corn furiously, tossing it into the pot. MEDEA enters.*]

MEDEA: Why are you doing that? I'm going to make dinner.

CHAC-MOOL: I'm not hungry.

MEDEA: Then what are you cooking for?

CHAC-MOOL: It's Luna's corn.

> [*She goes to the pot, lifts the lid.*]

MEDEA: It's blue.

CHAC-MOOL: Where is she? She doesn't even get to see it. She planted it. Why can't she see it? Why did you send her away?

MEDEA: I didn't send her away. She left.

CHAC-MOOL: You did. You made her unhappy. You make me unhappy. Stupid corn.

MEDEA: Chac-Mool.

CHAC-MOOL: The corn's ready to harvest. Bring her back.

MEDEA: I'm trying to save you, ingrato!

CHAC-MOOL: From what?

MEDEA: From . . . him.

CHAC-MOOL: You made Luna go away. He didn't.

MEDEA: To keep you.

CHAC-MOOL: To keep me for what?

MEDEA: For—

CHAC-MOOL: For yourself.

MEDEA: Yes. Is that such a crime? We can go back together, start all over again.

CHAC-MOOL: But I thought he didn't . . . You'd just leave her like that, Mom? After all this time? You don't even love him. Do you love him?

MEDEA: No.

CHAC-MOOL: Then?

MEDEA: Luna's found someone else, hijo.

CHAC-MOOL: I don't believe it.

MEDEA: Believe it.

CHAC-MOOL: But she loves you.

MEDEA: It's . . . hard. I . . .

[*CHAC-MOOL crosses to the pot and dumps out its contents.*]

CHAC-MOOL: You were a warrior woman, Mom. You were a fucking hero!

MEDEA: Chac . . .

CHAC-MOOL: What?

MEDEA: I'm almost fifty. I'm tired of fighting. I wanna go home.

[*Black out.*]

Scene Three

[*MEDEA stands in the kitchen. JASÓN enters, brushes aside the corn husks remaining on the kitchen table and places his briefcase down in their place.*]

MEDEA: I sent the papers back because they were unacceptable. You ignored my conditions.

JASÓN: You aren't in the position to negotiate, Medea.

MEDEA: I'm not?

JASÓN: Frankly, I think I'm being quite generous.

MEDEA: To live as your ward. I could stay here for that.

JASÓN: Semantics.

MEDEA: I know what "ward" means, Jasón.

JASÓN: It means I will take care of you. Your grandmother, too.

MEDEA: I'm not your Juárez whore, Señor. A woman is nothing in Aztlán without a husband.

JASÓN: Then stay here if you want. It's your decision.

MEDEA: Then we both stay. Chac-Mool's not going anywhere without me.

JASÓN: Medea, I don't want you.

MEDEA: And I don't want you, but I'm not going back to my land on my knees. I thought we gave up Catholicism with the revolution.

JASÓN: I'm in love with somebody else.

MEDEA: Love! You love a tight pussy around your dick, that's what you love. Why do you have to marry it? It will not make you younger.

JASÓN: Ah, Jeezus.

MEDEA: You raped me. Now pay up.

JASÓN: Oh, Medea. You orchestrated the whole damn thing.

MEDEA: When the prostitute is not paid as agreed, she is raped.

JASÓN: You said it. I never agreed to stay married to you.

MEDEA: She's a child in bed, you tell me. I want a woman. *(Mimicking him)* "I miss you. I miss your breasts, tu piel, that smell, how could I have gone so long without that smell."

JASÓN: It was the passion of the moment.

MEDEA: And the moment has passed.

JASÓN: . . . Yes.

MEDEA: Get out!

JASÓN: Not without my son!

MEDEA: ¿Qué crees? That you'll be free of me? I'll decide, not you. You'll never be free of me!

JASÓN: Free! You're the slave, Medea, not me. You will always be my woman because of our son. Whether you rot in this wasteland of counter-revolutionary degenerates or take up residence in my second bed. You decide. I'm not afraid of you, Medea. I used to be afraid of that anger, but not anymore. I have what I want now. Land and a future in the body of that boy. You can't stop me.

MEDEA: Watch me.

JASÓN: If you really loved your son, you'd remove him from your tit.

MEDEA: So his mouth can suck your dick?

JASÓN: That how your dyke friends talk, Medea? Look at you. You hate men. And boys become men. What good are you for Chac now? He needs a father.

MEDEA: My son needs no taste of that weakness you call manhood. He is still a boy, not a man and you will not make him one in your likeness! The man I wish my son to be does not exist, must be invented. He will invent himself if he must, but he will not grow up to learn betrayal from your example.

JASÓN: You left me.

MEDEA: And you sent away your son and his mother to live in exile.

JASÓN: You would not be separated.

MEDEA: That's one version of the story, Jasón. Would you like to hear the other? Or do you believe your own mythology? The "Minister of Culture" marrying una niñita. !Qué conveniente!

JASÓN: It's hardly convenient, Medea. I've had to defend this relationship—

MEDEA: She'll never call you by your true name, Jasón, so you may fortunately begin to forget it. Forget the U.S. Air Force father, the quarter-breed mestizo-de-mestizo cousins, your mother's coveted Spanish coat-of-arms. That girl can't know you because your lies were sown long before she made root on this earth. Send me your wife. I will teach her of her own embattled and embittered history. I will teach her, as I have learned, to defend women and children against enemies from within. Against fathers and brothers and sons who grow up to be as conquistador as any Cortez—

JASÓN: Oh, please.

MEDA: Traídores de una cultura mas anciana que your pitiful ego'd life can remember.

JASÓN: That bitterness in you . . . you'll never change.

MEDEA: Oh yes, I've changed. I married you when I was still a girl, not a woman, but a girl with a girl's naiveté who still looked for a father's protection. But that was a long time ago. I am a woman. A Mexican woman and there is no protection and no place for me, not even in the arms of another woman because she too is an exile in her own land. Marry your child-bride. A mi no me importa. No, in that lies no traición. Betrayal occurs when a boy grows into a man and sees his mother as a woman for the first time. A woman. A thing. A creature to be controlled.

JASÓN: If it is so inevitable, give me the boy. Spare yourself the humiliation.

MEDEA: No, my son is still an innocent. He will love you in spite of me, for his body requires that that animal memory be fulfilled. To that I do not object, nor to the fact that he must one day grow away from me, but he will leave me as a daughter does, with all the necessary wrenching, and his eye will never see me "as woman." I promise you that.

[*JASÓN opens his briefcase, takes out a document, puts it on the table.*]

JASÓN: The courts have already made their decision, Medea.

MEDEA: Which courts? Those patriarchs who stole my country? I returned to my motherland in the embrace of a woman and the mother is taken from me.

JASÓN: You agreed. Age thirteen. You signed the—

MEDEA: My hand was forced.

JASÓN: Bueno, the sundance starts in a matter of weeks. I'll be back for the . . . (*Spying CHAC-MOOL entering*) Adolfo . . .

CHAC-MOOL: My name's Chac-Mool. It's written on my arm, so I won't forget.

MEDEA: Hijo . . .

JASÓN: Chac-Mool, yes. You're . . . big.

[*CHAC-MOOL's eyes study JASÓN.*]

MEDEA: Tell him the truth, Jasón. Since my son is standing here in front of you, tell him to his face.

JASÓN: What are you talking about?

MEDEA: That my son makes you legit, just like I did. That's why you've suddenly appeared on our doorstep con tus papeles in hand.

CHAC-MOOL: Mom . . .

MEDEA: He is your native claim. You can't hold onto a handful of dirt in Aztlán without him. You don't have the blood quantum.

JASÓN: I'm a practical man, Medea.

MEDEA: I believe the word is opportunist.

JASÓN: Yes, there is that requirement, but that says nothing about my love for my son.

MEDEA: That's right. It says nothing.

JASÓN: There are the custody papers, Medea. The divorce is already a done deal. There's really nothing more to discuss. Chac-Mool, regardless of what your mother has said to you, I want to be with you. I admit, it's taken me a long time to . . . to grow up. I never should've let you go, but I'm coming back for you now. Once these papers are . . . taken care of, I hope you'll—

CHAC-MOOL: What?

JASÓN: Come home.

CHAC-MOOL: I . . . *(CHAC-MOOL looks over to MEDEA. Their eyes meet.)*

JASÓN: Bueno . . . *(JASÓN closes up his briefcase, leaving the documents on the table.)*

MEDEA: Get out.

JASÓN: Don't make this harder—

MEDEA: Get. Out.

JASÓN: Fine. Good-bye, Chac-Mool.

CHAC-MOOL: Bye.

> *[JASÓN exits. MEDEA goes to CHAC-MOOL.]*

MEDEA: Chac-Mool.

CHAC-MOOL: I barely remember him.

MEDEA: I'm sorry you had to see this.

CHAC-MOOL: Him?

MEDEA: Yes.

CHAC-MOOL: He's old. Small.

MEDEA: Yes.

CHAC-MOOL: Why didn't you tell me he was coming?

MEDEA: He brought papers. It was business.

CHAC-MOOL: About me.

MEDEA: I never would've let you go. Así. Without time to prepare.

CHAC-MOOL: Mom, I've been preparing.

MEDEA: I mean in your heart.

CHAC-MOOL: How do you do that?

MEDEA: I'm not sure.

CHAC-MOOL: I didn't know he even wanted me.

MEDEA: Didn't you hear him?

CHAC-MOOL: He wants me.

MEDEA: He wants you for a piece of dirt! He didn't deny it!

CHAC-MOOL: You didn't tell me.

MEDEA: He's using you! Just like he used me and when he's done with you, he'll toss you back here like so much basura.

CHAC-MOOL: Why you talking like this? Let's just go, take Bisabuela. There's nothing left for us here. You said so yourself.

MEDEA: I can't go.

CHAC-MOOL: Why not?

MEDEA: Nothing's changed, Chac-Mool. They want a public disavowal.

CHAC-MOOL: A what?

MEDEA: I can't deny what I am, hijo. I thought I could, but I can't.

CHAC-MOOL: He doesn't want you, does he? That's why.

MEDEA: Did you just hear what I said?

CHAC-MOOL: I want to be initiated, Mamá.

MEDEA: You want to cut open your chest?

CHAC-MOOL: No, I—

MEDEA: Is that what this is all about! Toma! *(Grabbing a letter opener from the table.)* Then start your initiation right here. Cut open your mother's chest first! Dig out her heart with your hands because that's what they'll teach you, to despise a mother's love, a woman's touch—

CHAC-MOOL: I won't do that.

MEDEA: You say that because you're still young. Your manhood, the size of acorns. When you feel yourself grown and hard as oak, you'll forget.

CHAC-MOOL: I won't forget. I'll come visit you. I promise.

MEDEA: *(Bitterly)* You'll visit.

CHAC-MOOL: I gotta get outta here. I can't do this no more, Mom. I'm just a kid, it's not normal!

MEDEA: You want normal? Then go with your father. He's perfectly normal. It's normal to send your five-year-old child and his mother into exile and then seven years later come back to collect the kid like a piece of property. It's normal for a nearly sixty-year-old Mexican man to marry a teenager. It's normal to lie about your race, your class, your origins, create a completely unoriginal fiction about yourself and then name yourself la patria's poet. But that's normal for a country that robs land from its daughters to give to its sons unless of course they turn out to be jotos.

CHAC-MOOL: Stop it, Mom. I don't wanna hear no more.

MEDEA: Well, I've got more to say!

CHAC-MOOL: No, not to me, you don't.

[He exits the kitchen.]

Scene Four

[Crossfade to the "Interrogation Room." CHAC-MOOL sits beneath a glaring spotlight. THE PRISON GUARD circles around him, holding a clipboard.]

BORDER GUARD: What is your name?

CHAC-MOOL: Adolfo.

BORDER GUARD: *(Checking the notes on the clipboard)* What about Chac-Mool?

CHAC-MOOL: If you knew already, why did you ask me?

BORDER GUARD: For the record.

CHAC-MOOL: For the record, my real name is Adolfo.

BORDER GUARD: And Chac-Mool?

CHAC-MOOL: It's my mom's name for me. It's written in my skin. You wanna see?

BORDER GUARD: No, they don't approve of graffiti en Aztlán. They do murals.

CHAC-MOOL: It's not—

BORDER GUARD: Let's get back to Adolfo, shall we? For the record.

CHAC-MOOL: For the record, I hate that name. It's a Nazi name. Every kid named Chuy has to live up to the legacy of being named Jesus. Well, me, I got Adolfo to follow me into the grave.

BORDER GUARD: Who named you?

CHAC-MOOL: My father, after some revolutionary, long-dead gun-runner uncle of his. But it's still a Nazi name. Sure there are other Adolphs in history . . . plenty of them, including my revolutionary uncle, but nobody with an impact even close to that of Hitler or Christ. I was born to be a Nazi, to have a Nazi life, to be denied a free life. Is nobody listening to me?

BORDER GUARD: We all are. It's your play.

CHAC-MOOL: Who says?

BORDER GUARD: You're the source of conflict. You're also the youngest one here, which means you're the future, it's gotta be about you. *And*, you're the only real male in the cast.

CHAC-MOOL: And who are you?

BORDER GUARD: Think of me as your revolutionary conscience, the mirror to that elegant Yaqui body of yours, inside and out.

CHAC-MOOL: Is this about a confession?

BORDER GUARD: What do you mean?

CHAC-MOOL: Like are you trying to get some kind of confession outta me.

BORDER GUARD: I'm trying to ascertain your readiness to make the return.

CHAC-MOOL: I don't want to be here no more.

BORDER GUARD: Where?

CHAC-MOOL: Tamoachán.

BORDER GUARD: Phoenix?

CHAC-MOOL: Yes.

BORDER GUARD: Where do you want to be?

CHAC-MOOL: Aztlán.

BORDER GUARD: Right answer. Tu patria.

CHAC-MOOL: Sí, mi patria. I am my father's son. I've got a right to be there. He tried to deny me. I was born from the sweat between my mother's thighs. He wanted to forget those campesina thighs.

BORDER GUARD: Who told you that?

CHAC-MOOL: My mother.

BORDER GUARD: And now?

CHAC-MOOL: And now . . . what?

BORDER GUARD: What does he want now?

CHAC-MOOL: Well, now he wants me back. To make a man outta me, to keep the Indian in him.

BORDER GUARD: He's not an Indian?

CHAC-MOOL: Not enough, according to my mother.

BORDER GUARD: And that's a problem?

CHAC-MOOL: In Aztlán it is. God, I thought you knew the place.

BORDER GUARD: Not really. I hardly remember. I only work the border. And what do you want outta the deal?

CHAC-MOOL: The return?

BORDER GUARD: Yes.

CHAC-MOOL: I just don't wanna have to hurt nobody.

BORDER GUARD: Nazi, let me introduce myself.

CHAC-MOOL: You said it was my play.

BORDER GUARD: You want this play?

CHAC-MOOL: I don't know yet. I don't know if I want you in it. I know I don't want you to be a man. Men scare me.

BORDER GUARD: Your father's a man.

CHAC-MOOL: I got nowhere else to go.

BORDER GUARD: I'll be a woman.

CHAC-MOOL: Be my mother. I miss my mother. I'm leaving her.

BORDER GUARD: No, not your mother. I am your revolutionary con-science. Today using modern methods I could convince you of anything. That you are no more than your father's son. The son del nuevo patrón revolucionario, a landowner from whom you will inherit property and a legacy of blood under the fingernails. Today using modern methods, I am landless. A woman without a country. I am she whom you already know to hate. I wipe your infant ass in another life, sensitive Nazi-boy.

CHAC-MOOL: *(Rising)* I've had enough of this.

BORDER GUARD: *(Pushing him down again, hand on his shoulder)* It's cold out. Where could you possibly go in such weather? It's too hot to move.

CHAC-MOOL: I have a country. I am not despised as you are. There is a piece of dirt a few hundred miles away from here that still holds the impression of my footsteps. I belong somewhere. I am going.

BORDER GUARD: Footsteps, the size of boys' feet?

CHAC-MOOL: I am not ready to be a man.

BORDER GUARD: No?

CHAC-MOOL: I was always blessed to be a boy. My great-grandmother literally traced my forehead with the cross of her thumb and index finger and my brow was tranquil then. I didn't then have these violent thoughts of a man. At four, my father drilled his fingers into my chest, held me at the gun point of his glare. You are blessed, he told me. Open your nostrils and flare like a bull. I want you to smell this land. I remember the wings of my nostrils rising up to suck up his breath. It was a birthing of sorts. He penetrated and I was born of him. His land was his mother and mine and I was beholden only to it.

BORDER GUARD: Aztlán.

CHAC-MOOL: Yes, Aztlán. And then my mother stole me away with the stonemason. A sculptor.

BORDER GUARD: Get up now.

CHAC-MOOL: *(Standing)* Did I pass? Am I ready?

BORDER GUARD: We caught you just in time. *(CHAC-MOOL exits, the GUARD announces:)* Too late. La Despedida.

Scene Five

> *[Crossfade to LUNA who is on her knees, putting various hand tools into a burlap tool bag. MEDEA stands a distance from her.]*

MEDEA: Stop it.

LUNA: What?

MEDEA: Stop packing.

LUNA: I need my tools.

MEDEA: That's why you came?

LUNA: You told me to come get them.

MEDEA: No seas terca.

LUNA: *(Stands, approaches MEDEA)* Then?

MEDEA: Then what?

LUNA: Then say it. Say what is hardest to say.

MEDEA: I would've respected you more, had you just left. You don't have the courage to be alone. You'll flop from woman to woman for the rest of your life.

LUNA: That's not it. That wasn't hard. Try again.

MEDEA: *(Softening)* I had a dream.

LUNA: Good.

MEDEA: I dreamed our land returned to us.

LUNA: Go on.

MEDEA: You were there. It was the most natural evolution in the world to move from love of country to love of you.

LUNA: And—

MEDEA: There was a road of yellow dust, sagüaro and maguey. You were laying down the cactus stones one by one to my door.

LUNA: Why did you shut the door, Medea?

MEDEA: My son.

LUNA: No. The truth.

MEDEA: My son.

LUNA: Look. *(She reaches into her pocket and pulls out a handful of blue corn kernels. She holds them out to MEDEA.)* The corn is going to seed.

MEDEA: Ya lo sé.

LUNA: I tried to warn you, Medea.

MEDEA: Fucking means nothing!

LUNA: It means something to me.

MEDEA: And your negra?

LUNA: She's a friend.

MEDEA: A friend!

LUNA: You're right. I don't want to be alone. Not now. I couldn't bear it.

MEDEA: I sacrificed Aztlán for you!

LUNA: Aztlán was uninhabitable.

[LUNA *finishes packing the bag, stands.*]

MEDEA: And the boy. . . ?

LUNA: We could never keep him here. I wouldn't want to.

[LUNA *exits. MEDEA pours herself a shot of tequila, downs it. BORDER GUARD enters with Mama Sal's satchel and dumps dozens of small plastic bags of herbs from it onto the kitchen table. She exits. MEDEA becomes frenzied, nervously searching through the bags. She sniffs the contents of one, then discards it, tries another and another. She finally finds the one she is looking for, tastes it gingerly with a wet fingertip, attempts to pour it into a measuring cup, but spills it, her hands shaking uncontrollably. She downs another shot of tequila.]*

Scene Six

[MAMA SAL sits outside smoking a pipe. CHAC-MOOL enters, carrying a small backpack.]

MAMA SAL: You should've called me. I would've met you at the bus station.

CHAC-MOOL: That's all right.

MAMA SAL: I love the bus station. Everybody goin' someplace. Are you going, hijo?

CHAC-MOOL: Yeah. Just came to get my stuff. Say good-bye.

MAMA SAL: Who knows? Maybe I'll even follow you there in a few years.

CHAC-MOOL: I'd like that.

MAMA SAL: It don't matter no more. Lesbiana ni lesbiana. I have outlived all the lovely womans in my life. *(Pause)* You do me un favor, Chaco?

CHAC-MOOL: Dígame.

MAMA SAL: If I don't get back there, you don't let them bury me here, eh?

CHAC-MOOL: I won't, Bisabuela.

MAMA SAL: Just fire me up como un cigaro and put me en tu bolsillo—

CHAC-MOOL: I'm not gonna do that!

MAMA SAL: I mean it. And take me out there by those ruinas . . . out there en las montañas de Jemez.

CHAC-MOOL: I don't know where that is.

MAMA SAL: You'll find out. Just spread me around out there with all that red rock. I'm tired of this pinche city.

CHAC-MOOL: I promise.

MAMA SAL: Bueno. *(She gets up, putting her pipe in her pocket.)* Oh, mira. Luna came by. She wanted me to give you these.

[She takes out a small bag of corn kernels from her pocket, hands them to CHAC-MOOL.]

CHAC-MOOL: They're from the garden?

MAMA SAL: Uh-huh. She thought maybe you could throw a few kernels over there in Nuevo México, see if they take root.

CHAC-MOOL: Did she see my Mom?

MAMA SAL: Yep.

CHAC-MOOL: She gone?

MAMA SAL: Sí. Tools y todo.

[With some difficulty, MAMA SAL starts to get up from the chair. CHAC-MOOL goes to help her.]

MAMA SAL: Go on in there now, talk to your Mamá. *(She kisses him on the cheek.)*

CHAC-MOOL: You're not coming?

MAMA SAL: Hell no. Talking about my own damn burial, I'm gointu go find me some beer.

[She exits. CHAC-MOOL crosses to the cornfield and throws the kernels back into it. Lights fade out.]

Scene Seven

[CHAC-MOOL enters the kitchen where MEDEA is sitting with the tequila and herbs laid out in front of her.]

MEDEA: I tried getting her back. But I wouldn't beg. If you expected me to beg, I didn't.

CHAC-MOOL: I didn't expect nothing.

MEDEA: You been to the border?

CHAC-MOOL: Yes.

MEDEA: Then go pack your bags.

CHAC-MOOL: Mom.

MEDEA: You've decided, haven't you? You've been approved.

CHAC-MOOL: Yes.

MEDEA: Then go pack your bags.

CHAC-MOOL: I don't wanna leave you like this.

MEDEA: Now, that's a line I've heard before. But they leave you anyway, don't they, the line-givers?

CHAC-MOOL: It's not a line.

MEDEA: They're all lines, mijito. Rehearsed generations in advance and transmitted into your little male DNA.

CHAC-MOOL: Why you turning on me, Mom?

MEDEA: I think that's the question I have to ask you.

CHAC-MOOL: What am I supposed to do? Who am I supposed to be, Mom? There's nobody to be. No man to be.

MEDEA: So all the tíos I've surrounded you with aren't men.

CHAC-MOOL: That's not what I mean.

MEDEA: Jotos aren't men.

CHAC-MOOL: They're not my father.

MEDEA: You are not the first boy in the world to grow up without a father.

CHAC-MOOL: And without a country? You made me want it, Mom, more than anything. It was "our blood got spilled. Yaqui blood." That's what you said to me every day, every day like a prayer. I can't help it that they took Aztlán away from you.

MEDEA: But you'll take it away again, won't you?

CHAC-MOOL: How?

MEDEA: *(Grabbing him by the shoulders.)* You're my land, hijo. Don't you see that? You're my land!

CHAC-MOOL: How is that any different from my father?

MEDEA: Chinga'o! Because I am the Indian, not him! And I am your mother!

CHAC-MOOL: That's not my fault!

[She freezes.]

MEDEA: I've held my breath for thirteen years in fear of hearing those words come out of your mouth, to hear you finally absolve yourself of me!

CHAC-MOOL: But what did I do? You chose to leave Aztlán! You chose for yourself, not for me!

MEDEA: That's right. I chose Luna. Remember Luna?

CHAC-MOOL: I remember. Where is she now?

[MEDEA crosses back to the table. Takes a shot, she keeps her back to him.]

CHAC-MOOL: That's it? You're not gonna talk to me no more?

MEDEA: You win. Vete.

[He doesn't move.]

MEDEA: Go, Chac-Mool.

[He doesn't.]

MEDEA: *(Turning to him)* What? You want my blessing, too? ¡Qué dios te bendiga! Lo siento mucho, hijo, pero no soy tu madre dadivosa. *(Grabbing her breast)* The chichi has run dry.

CHAC-MOOL: You're crazy. He's right. He told me you were crazy. He met me at the border. He told me to come with him right then.

MEDEA: You should have.

CHAC-MOOL: I didn't. I didn't because you taught me loyalty. Because I wasn't going to sneak away from you like a punk. When I leave here tomorrow, I'm walking out that door like a man.

MEDEA: A man.

CHAC-MOOL: Yeah, a man. Just the way you taught me. You fucked him, I didn't. You fucked yourself.

[MEDEA slaps CHAC-MOOL. He stares at her, half in disdain, half in pity. He exits. MEDEA slumps onto the chair at the kitchen table. She reaches again for the herbs, fingers them. MAMA SAL appears at the doorway, a sack of beer in her hands.]

MAMA SAL: ¿Qúe pasó? ¿Qué 'stás haciendo?

[MEDEA lets the herbs run through her fingers.]

MEDEA: All the babies, they're slipping through my fingers now. I can't stop them. They've turned into the liquid of the river and they are drowning in my hands.

MAMA SAL: Medea . . .

MEDEA: I lost my baby. We were splintered, severed in two. I wanted a female to love, that's all, Abuelita. Is that so much to want?

MAMA SAL: No.

MEDEA: *(Holding up a bag full of herbs)* How much?

MAMA SAL: No, Medea. You don't have to do this.

MEDEA: A stranger has inhabited me, taken possession of my body, disguised himself innocently in the sexless skin of my placenta. *(Extending the bag to her)* How much?

MAMA SAL: Half of that. Es suficiente.

[MEDEA *dumps the herbs into a pot as the lights crossfade to* CIHUATATEO *entering as women warriors. They perform a stylized enactment of a traditional midwife birthing. There is chanting in Nahuatl and deep moaning. NURSE stands between MEDEA's legs awaiting the birth. As the infant emerges, we see that it is LUNA, in the lifeless form of a woman. She is shapeless liquid. The others cannot revive her. They all scatter, leave her abandoned on stage, except for* CIHUATATEO WEST, *who as the lights change, takes on the shape of* SAVANNAH. *She draws a huge white sheet over LUNA and herself. When the couple re-emerge, they are joined together in the sack of sheet. It is a kind of tableau of the Aztec codex, symbolizing marriage. THE PRISON GUARD enters.]*

PRISON GUARD: "Blood Wedding."

LUNA: Medea was pregnant. Within weeks she knew and the matter of names came up again, what to call that he/she clinging fish-gilled and hermaphrodite inside her liquid belly. She loved her belly more than any man but was grateful to Jasón for that first effortless conception. He had once taken her, virginal and spineless. Except there was no blood, no stain upon the sheet. The blood was only under her tongue, I found. A small pool behind the bottom row of her teeth, a dam holding back the ruby kiss, the original name of which she once spilled into my mouth. I, who would never give her children. I, who would always make her sweat and bleed every month. Our shared moons, a marriage of the most bitter, sweet-lipped kind.

SAVANNAH: Just keep talkin' that talk, girl, and I'll never leave you.

[SAVANNAH pulls LUNA back down under the sheet. Black out.]

Scene Eight

[As in the beginning of the play, the figure of Coatlicue is illuminated. MEDEA, wearing a long white nightgown, stands before the statue in prayer, holding a cup in her hand. She raises it in offering to the Diosa.]

MEDEA:
Coatlicue,
this is my holy sacrifice.

I would have preferred to die a warrior woman,
like the Cihuatateo
women who die in childbirth
offering their own lives
to the birthing of others.

How much simpler things would have been.
But what life do I have to offer to my son now?

He refuses my gifts and turns to my enemies
to make a man of him.
I cannot relinquish my son to them,
to walk ese camino triste
where they will call him
by his manly name
and he goes deaf
to hear it.

But the road I must walk is sadder still.

[CHAC-MOOL enters. MEDEA turns to him, a bit off guard.]

CHAC-MOOL: I know it's stupid, but . . . I just came in to say good night.

MEDEA: You going to bed already?

CHAC-MOOL: Yeah, it's a long trip tomorrow.

MEDEA: *(After a beat)* Forgive me, hijo.

CHAC-MOOL: Mom, I—

MEDEA: Ya. Tal vez no vale mucho after so many words, harsh words, pero . . . could I bless you now, before you go?

CHAC-MOOL: Now?

MEDEA: I got the copal burning.

CHAC-MOOL: Okay.

> [He goes to her, opens his hands in front of him. She brings the smoking resin to him, wafts his body with it.]

MEDEA: Our ancestors are watching, hijo. They pity us. They know what is in our hearts.

CHAC-MOOL: I'm . . . sorry.

> [She prays over him softly, then returns the burning copal to her altar.]

MEDEA: Can you stay up with your mami for a little while?

CHAC-MOOL: I'm tired, Mom.

MEDEA: I made you some atole. It may not be as good as Luna's, pero no quieres probarlo? I made it with the blue corn.

CHAC-MOOL: Sure.

MEDEA: Vete. Go put on your pijamas first. Yo te espero.

CHAC-MOOL: Okay.

> [CHAC-MOOL starts to exit, then suddenly turns and runs over to her. He throws his arms around MEDEA. MEDEA starts to pull him away and he clings all the tighter.]

CHAC-MOOL: I love you, Mom.

MEDEA: Sí, hijo. Ya lo sé. Now, go get changed, then come outside. You can drink your atole out there. The moon is so bright.

CHAC-MOOL: Okay.

[*CHAC-MOOL exits. MEDEA takes out a bag of herbs from her gown, sprinkles them into the atole. She addresses COATLICUE.*]

MEDEA: Can you smell it, Madre? Mi hijo's manhood. He wears it in his sleep now. In the morning I find it in a heap on the floor, crumpled in his pijamas. Like Luna, I bring the soft flannel to my nose. I inhale. No baby smell. No boy. A man moving inside his body. I felt a small rise against my thigh just now, a small beating heart hardening against that place that was once his home. Where is my baby's sweet softness now?

[*CHAC-MOOL re-enters, naked from the waist up and wearing pajama pants. MEDEA holds the cup of atole.*]

CHAC-MOOL: Mom?

MEDEA: Vente, hijo. It's too hot in here. Let's go watch the corn grow.

[*She grabs his hand and escorts him outside into the backyard, next to the field of corn. They sit down together, She puts her arms around him.*]

MEDEA: El maíz 'stá muy alto.

CHAC-MOOL: Yeah, too tall. I feel kind of bad I didn't harvest it.

MEDEA: No te apures. In Aztlán, there's plenty corn to harvest.

[*MEDEA offers CHAC-MOOL the atole.*]

MEDEA: Toma, hijo. This will help you sleep. *(He drinks.)*

CHAC-MOOL: Mom—

MEDEA: Don't say anything more, hijo. No mas palabras.

[MEDEA takes CHAC-MOOL into her arms. She rocks him, singing.]

MEDEA:

> *Duérmete mi niño*
> *Duérmete mi sol*
> *Duérmete pedazo*
> *de mi corazón.*

My sleeping hombrecito. *(He is instantly drowsy. She strokes his hair.)* Sleep, mi diosito. Sleep the innocent sleep of the childless.

[He passes out. It is a pieta image, MEDEA holding him limp within her arms. Then, with much effort, she tries to drag CHAC-MOOL's body into the small field of corn. She is unable to. The CIHUATATEO enter, dressed in the traditional Aztec. They lift CHAC-MOOL and take him into the center of the field. Meanwhile, MEDEA starts pulling up all the overgrown corn stalks in the field, piling them into a mound higher and higher. She becomes frenzied, a frightening image, her white nightgown flowing in the sudden wind. The pile of blue corn stalks have formed a kind of altar. The CIHUATATEO heave CHAC-MOOL's body on top of it.]

MEDEA:
Hijo! Mensajero!
How much simpler had you been born a daughter
that first female seed inside of me.
You would have comforted me in old age
held vigil at the hour of my death
washed my body with sweet soap
anointing it with oil.

You would have wrapped me in colored cloths
worthy of the meeting of mothers.
My finest feathers and skins would adorn me
as you returned me to the earth.

[Calling out against the wind and to the illuminated figure of Coatlicue.]

What crime do I commit now, Mamá?
To choose the daughter over the son?

You betrayed us, Madre Coatlicue.
You, anciana, you who birthed the God of War.

Huitzilopotchli.
His Aztec name sours upon my lips,
as the name of the son
of the woman who gave me birth.

My mother did not stop my brother's hand
from reaching into my virgin bed.
Nor did you hold back the sword
that severed your daughter's head.

Coyolxauhqui, diosa de la luna.
[Her arms stretch out to the full moon.]
Ahora, she is my god.
La Luna, la hija rebelde.

Te rechazo, Madre.

MEDEA: ¡AY-Y-Y-Y! ¡MI HI-I-I-I-J0!

[THE CIHUATATEO echo her.]

CIHUATATEO: ¡MIS HI-I-I-I-J0S!

[Their lament is accompanied by the soft cry of the wind in the background that swells into a deep moaning. It is the cry of La Llorona. The moon moves behind the mountains. The lights fade to black.]

Epilogue

[Flauta and tambor. The CIHUATATEO NORTH and SOUTH appear upstage. They are positioned together in the statuesque pose of the original icons: kneeling, sitting on their heels, their hands pushed forward in a kind of martial arts stance. They begin to dance in slow ritualized movement. Lights rise on LUNA who sits before a potter's wheel. She leans into a mass of clay. Mama Sal's satchel sits at her feet.]

LUNA:

> In her absence she is all the disguises she wore. She is
> the flood of fever that fills my veins
> with a woman's passing perfume. She is
> la música flamenca, the gypsy allure,
> the lie.

> She is the painting of a woman fractured and defiant.
> Cueva of clay opening como flor.
> Coyolxauhqui's unnamed star sister. She is

> renegade rebozo, el tambor's insistence,
> a warrior's lament.
> Slender hips of silk.
> She is silk.

> *[Moving more deeply into the clay with her hands]*

> I could sing of her breasts with my hands.

> With my hands, I could sing
> she was a woman who never stopped being naked to me.

> *[LUNA rises. The PRISON GUARD enters, helps LUNA put on a suit jacket, hands her a bouquet of fresh white flowers and Mama Sal's satchel. She escorts LUNA to the psychiatric ward. The PRISON GUARD joins the CIHUATATEO upstage. MEDEA waits on the edge of her bed.]*

LUNA: Medea?

MEDEA: *(She does not look at LUNA)* You've come back. I thought you'd never come back.

LUNA: I was stopped at the border.

MEDEA: *(Turning to her)* It must be Saturday. Again.

LUNA: Yes, it's Saturday.

MEDEA: Thank you for the flowers. *(She doesn't take them.)* How is my grandmother?

LUNA: She's old, Medea. Old and tired.

MEDEA: She should be less tired now. I was a burden to her.

LUNA: Yes. How are you?

MEDEA: I'm old and tired, I think, too. *(She crosses to the window)*

LUNA: I dreamed of you last night.

MEDEA: I thought so.

LUNA: In the image of a maguey exploding from a vagina.

MEDEA: More flowers?

LUNA: No, desert cactus. There was nothing sweet about it.

MEDEA: *(Turning to her)* You know what I always loved about you, Luna?

LUNA: No, what?

MEDEA: Your innocence.

LUNA: I'm . . . innocent?

[MEDEA *goes to her, wraps her hands around* LUNA's.]

MEDEA: Your hands. Your hands have handled dozens of women and somehow they remain virgin hands. You left her, didn't you?

LUNA: Who?

MEDEA: The other woman.

LUNA: . . . Yes.

MEDEA: Not me, I'm not innocent. I am spoiled. What I touch is spoiled and I am spoiled by the touches of others.

LUNA: Did I spoil you, Medea?

MEDEA: You said it yourself, you ruined me.

LUNA: I didn't mean—

MEDEA: *(Letting go of her)* You were right. You made me good for no one. Man, woman or child.

LUNA: I'm sorry.

> *[There is a pause.]*

MEDEA: Luna?

LUNA: Yes?

MEDEA: Was the vagina yours? In the dream?

LUNA: Maybe.

MEDEA: And I was the maguey?

LUNA: Maybe. Maybe it was all you. You giving birth to yourself.

> *[MEDEA smiles.]*

LUNA: I brought you something.

MEDEA: No more flowers, Luna. They remind me of death.

LUNA: No.

> *[She opens Mama Sal's bag and pulls out a small bundle.]*

MEDEA: You have Mama's bag.

LUNA: Toma.

> *[LUNA gives MEDEA the bundle. MEDEA unwraps it, stares at it, awed.]*

LUNA: It's a Cihuatateo.

MEDEA: *(Suddenly urgent)* Is that how I died, Luna? Giving birth to myself?

LUNA: I—

MEDEA: Is that what you came to tell me?

LUNA: I . . . don't know.

> [NURSE enters. MEDEA and LUNA eyes are locked onto each other.]

NURSE: You want me to put those flowers in some water, negra?

LUNA: What? No. She doesn't want them.

NURSE: But they're so gorgeous.

LUNA: Yes, you take them then. Put them in some water. They've been hours out of water.

NURSE: Chevere.

> [NURSE takes the flowers and exits. She joins the CORO of CIHUATATEO.]

MEDEA: Thank you.

LUNA: Sure.

MEDEA: Luna, go away now.

LUNA: You—

MEDEA: Please.

LUNA: Good bye, Medea.

> [LUNA leaves. MEDEA holds the Cihuatateo figure in her hands. She looks upstage to the CORO.]

CIHUATATEO:
>And though banished from Aztlán
>Medea and Luna kept the faith,
>fasted by the phases of the moon
>but did not pierce their flesh
>for they bled regularly between their legs
>and did not die.

[CHAC-MOOL suddenly appears in MEDEA's room.]

MEDEA: Are you a ghost?

CHAC-MOOL: No.

MEDEA: You're mistaken. You are a ghost. You're the son I mourn, the one I pray to, that his heart may soften when I join him on the other side.

CHAC-MOOL: It's me.

MEDEA: Daily, I try to join him and my hands are always emptied of the instruments of death. They steal my fingernail file and pantyhose and yerbas. They give me no yerbas here, just pathetic pastel pills that numb me, but won't kill me. They're useless.

CHAC-MOOL: Mother.

MEDEA: Mother. I had a mother once, for a moment. Do you have a mother?

CHAC-MOOL: Yes.

MEDEA: Is she beautiful? I imagine she's beautiful. You are beautiful or maybe you are the image of your father.

CHAC-MOOL: She's beautiful.

MEDEA: That's nice how you talk about her. I'd like to meet her. I love beautiful women, but it's best not to touch them too much. Touch yourself better, if you're beautiful. Another beautiful woman is hard to take sometimes for too long. It's confusing. I mean, for a woman. It's not confusing for a man. But you're not quite a man yet, not fully.

But it's coming. I can see it in your eyes. If you had been my son, the dark of your eyes would mirror me. And we would blend together sexless.

CHAC-MOOL: Mom, I'm Chac-Mool.

MEDEA: Chac-Mool. No.

CHAC-MOOL: It's true. I—

MEDEA: No, stop. Don't speak any more. Go away.

CHAC-MOOL: Mom, don't make me go.

MEDEA: If you live, then why am I here? I've committed no crime. If you live, why then am I strapped into the bed at night? Why am I plagued with nightmares of babies melting between my hands? Why do I mourn you and no longer walk the horizon at the hour of sunset as I used to? Why are there locks and I haven't the key? Why?

CHAC-MOOL: You're in a hospital. A prison.

MEDEA: An insane asylum?

CHAC-MOOL: Yes.

MEDEA: Then I am insane.

CHAC-MOOL: I don't know.

MEDEA: Oh. *(Pause)* Why have you come here?

CHAC-MOOL: To take you away.

MEDEA: Away . . . where?

CHAC-MOOL: Home.

MEDEA: Home. *(She stares ahead blankly.)*

CHAC-MOOL: Come look out the window, Mom. See the moon.

MEDEA: Yes. Nurse told me it's a nice afternoon. A beautiful woman brought me flowers today. Is today still Saturday?

CHAC-MOOL: Come here, Mom. ¿Ves la luna?

[CHAC-MOOL grabs his mother's hand, takes her to the small window.]

MEDEA: La Luna. That was her name.

CHAC-MOOL: Mom.

MEDEA: Mom. The sun is too bright.

CHAC-MOOL: No, mira. Do you see the moon? There to the left, just above those hills. *(She cranes her neck to see.)*

MEDEA: Oh yes. She's droopy-eyed.

CHAC-MOOL: No, she's waxing. Watch the moon. By the full moon, you'll be looking at saguaros. You're going home.

MEDEA: How will I get there?

CHAC-MOOL: I'm taking you.

[He leads her by the hand back to the bed. He holds a handful of powdered herbs and puts them into a small paper cup of water.]

MEDEA: Mijo?

CHAC-MOOL: Here, drink this. It'll help you sleep.

[CHAC-MOOL holds MEDEA's head while she drinks. She is instantly drowsy. CHAC-MOOL gathers her into his arms as she falls into a deep sleep. It is a pieta image.

The lights gradually fade. Only the shimmering moon remains, and the figure of the four CIHUATATEO dancing silently in its light.]

End of Play

heart of the earth
A Popol Vuh Story

Directed and Puppets by Ralph Lee
Book and Lyrics by Cherríe L. Moraga
Music by Glen Vélez

Heart of the Earth: A Popol Vuh Story, written by Cherríe L. Moraga, first opened on September 14, 1994 at The Public Theatre as part of the Jim Henson Foundation's International Festival of Puppet Theatre. The play was directed by Ralph Lee, who also created the puppets (from hand- to giant-sized), and the music was composed by Glen Velez. The opening included the following cast (in order of appearance):

DAYKEEPER/IXMUCANE/BAT	Doris Difarnecio
IXPIYACOC/BLOOD SAUSAGE	William Ha'o
CUCUMATZ/PATRIARCHAL PUS	Sam Wellington
HUNAHPU (Both generations)	Joe Herrera
VUCUB/OLLAS/IXBALANQUE	David Noroña
TECOLOTE/WOODEN-MAN/THE RAT	Julie Pasqual
IXQUIC/CONEJO	Adriana Inchaustegui

"Heart of the Earth" had its World Premiere at INTAR Theatre of New York on January 11, 1995. It opened with the following cast:

DAYKEEPER/IXMUCANE/BAT	Doris Difarnecio
IXPIYACOC/BLOOD SAUSAGE	William Ha'o
CUCUMATZ/PATRIARCHAL PUS	Curtis Cook
HUNAHPU (Both generations)	Joe Herrera
VUCUB/OLLAS/IXBALANQUE	David Noroña
TECOLOTE/WOODEN-MAN/THE RAT	Caroline Stephanie Clay
IXQUIC/CONEJO	Adriana Inchaustegui

Musicians were Iris Brooks and David Simons. Choreography by Sigfrido Aguilar. Set by Donald Eastman. Costumes by Caryn Neman. The Stage Manager was Jesse Wooden, Jr. and the Assistant Director, Laura Esparza.

Note from the Playwright

About the Language:
Heart of the Earth: A Popol Vuh Story is a multi-lingual, multi-cultural adaptation of the Quiché Maya creation myth. The language employed in the play includes standard English and Spanish, Quiché, other Mayan tongues, Spanglish, Chicano speech from the Southwest, and the urban colloquialisms of U.S. city streets. I have tried to create a version of the *Popol Vuh* that honors its original language, while acknowledging that Quiché is a living language used not only among the Maya in the highlands of Guatemala, but can also be heard on the streets of New York City, along with Quechua, Nahuatl, Navajo, Lakota, and a myriad of other Indigenous American tongues. As *Heart of the Earth* is being presented in the U.S., the world of language I hope to evoke is one of a diverse and people-of-color América that more closely reflects its changing and beautifully darkening face as we enter the 21st century.

Cherríe L. Moraga
New York City
July 7, 1994

The Set

The set of the world of *Heart of the Earth* features a Maya-style pyramid, where much of the action of the play takes place. The steps leading to the top of the pyramid become the highland cornfields (or milpas) where to this day Mayas cultivate maíz in tiers alongside the mountains. In the play the Corn God appears here to offer abundance to those who pray to the spirit. Steps leading down the pyramid represent the treacherous journey to Xibalba, the underworld where the Lords of Death reside. At the base of the pyramid is a small hutch-like opening which serves as the site of various ritual sacrifices, a miraculous birth, and a bat house jail cell.

When in the land of the gods, downstage right is reserved for the activities of the women. Here Grandmother works at her metate, grinding up maíz — the substance and sustenance for humankind, and Daughter-in-law embroiders, creating designs from her dreams. Stage left serves as the gods' "creation work-shop," where together Grandfather and Plumed Serpent attempt to create "Man" out of mud and wood.

At times the entire stage becomes a ball court, where the Twins play a ball game, the style of which, in the play, is drawn from the traditional Pre-Columbian version and mixed with a kind of contemporary soccer and basketball. In short, the set is versatile and the stark contrast between the world of the gods and the underworld is achieved through dramatic shifts in lighting and music.

The Characters

DAYKEEPER
IXMUCANE (Abuela, Grandmother)
IXPIYACOC (Abuelo, Grandfather)
CUCUMATZ (Huracan, Kukulcan, Bahana, La Culebra Verde,
    Plumed Serpent)
HUNAHPU (First-generation Twin)
VUCUB (First-generation Twin)
TECOLOTE (Owl)
PATRIARCHAL PUS (Lord of Death)
BLOOD SAUSAGE (Lord of Death)
IXQUIC (Blood Woman, Mother of the second-generation twins)
HUNAHPU (2nd-generation Twin)
IXBALANQUE (2nd-generation Twin)
RAT
WOODEN-MAN
OLLAS (Pots)
CONEJO (Rabbit)
THE CORN PEOPLE/DANCERS

Scene One

[The conch shell sounds. DAYKEEPER appears. Two large cloths rest on the floor of an otherwise bare stage. A pyramid is illuminated upstage.]

DAYKEEPER: This is the root de la palabra anciana, in a place named Quiché. Es la raíz de un pueblo of earth and sky that we shall plant here in the hearts of its descendants. This is the story of how light was born from darkness y la luz shadowed again by the hands of the gods. We shall tell our cuento en voz alta for there is no place to read it.

[Music: "Conquistadores"]

Five hundred years ago, the bearded ones arrived in floating palacios, in search of the sun's golden secretions. They came armed with flechas of melded steel and a black book decrying their devil. *(Pause)* Today our children know fewer and fewer Indian prayers; they put on the Ladino cloth of soldier and seller. And our book and its author keep their faces hidden.

[IXPIYACOC enters carrying a god-headdress, gives it to DAYKEEPER who immediately puts it on, becoming IXMUCANE.]

IXMUCANE: Gracias, Abuelo.

[They pick up the cloths and begin to manipulate them in a kind of dance. The sky-earth are created.]

IXPIYACOC: In the beginning, there was just sea and sky.

IXMUCANE: Nothing stirred.

IXPIYACOC: Uleu was a breath held back,

IXMUCANE: a speechless sea,

LOS ABUELOS: kissing the limitless sky.

LOS ABUELOS: *(Chanting)*
    ucah tzucuxic
    ucah xucutaxic
        retaxic,
    ucah cheexic,

    umeh camaxic,
    uyuc camaxic

    upa cah,
    upa uleu

    cah tzuc
    cah xucut

[Music transition. CUCUMATZ emerges from inside the cloth. The green-blue PLUMED SERPENT dances majestically in a dramatic opening.]

IXMUCANE: Cucumatz!

IXPIYACOC: You are named by your queztal-feathered splendor.

IXMUCANE: Kukulcan.

IXPIYACOC: La Culebra Verde.

IXMUCANE: Nao'tsiti.

IXPIYACOC: Plumed Serpent.

IXMUCANE: Culebra Fuerte y Sabia.

IXPIYACOC: Bahana.

IXMUCANE: Corazón del Cielo.

IXPIYACOC: Huracan!

[*LOS ABUELOS join CUCUMATZ in the dance. They mark and measure the four directions, the four corners of the universe, stretching and folding the cloth, as if preparing a cornfield for planting. Counting out their footsteps in dance, they chant as they work, creating the site where the story of the Popol Vuh will unfold.*]

The East, the place where the sun is born.
The South, el Mundo Tamanco.
The West, the place where the sun passes into darkness.
The North, el Mundo Pipil.

[*The four directions named, CUCUMATZ ascends the pyramid.*]

Scene Two

[*Lighting transition. Music: "The World of the Gods." LOS ABUELOS join CUCUMATZ on the pyramid.*]

IXPIYACOC: This will not do at all. I am thoroughly bored. There's nothing to look at. No people, no animals, no trees, not a blade of grass. No tenemos pájaros, ni cangrejos. We have no stones, no straw, no seed and no flowers.

IXMUCANE: What are you complaining about, viejo.

IXPIYACOC: *(Startled)* ¿Mande?

IXMUCANE: You're talking to yourself.

IXPIYACOC: Oh, it's just that at times, I get a little frustrated, tú sabes. There's so much in my mind and so little made manifest.

IXMUCANE: We have our sons.

IXPIYACOC: Sí, pero I have a world of ideas, corazón.

IXMUCANE: Paciencia, querido. The time draws near for all that.

CUCUMATZ: Tienes razón, comadre. It is time to proceed with the creation of the world. ¿Están listos?

IXPIYACOC: *(A bit amazed)* Listos. Sí. Estamos muy listos.

CUCUMATZ: Bueno. *(He gets into a meditation posture. Meditation music rises in the background.)* Just think about it.

[They sit for a moment in silence. CUCUMATZ and IXMUCANE begin to chant softly.]

IXMUCANE and CUCUMATZ:
    Keh, Tz'ikin, Koh, Balam, Kumatz
    Pa k'im, Pa zaq'ul, Pa k'icheelah.

IXPIYACOC: *(Confused)* Excuse me, Plumed Serpent, but . . . think about what?

CUCUMATZ: Piénsenlo and the creation shall begin.

[CUCUMATZ and IXMUCANE begin to chant again. IXPIYACOC joins them. Sound and light effects, the creation of the earth is taking place.]

    Keh, Tz'ikin, Koh, Balam, Kumatz
    Pa k'im, Pa zaq'ul, Pa k'icheelah.

IXMUCANE: I see it. I see the water receding, separating from the earth.

[Sound builds upon sound, beginning with a single stream of water, then the sound of animals, emerging one after the other, squawking and squeaking.]

IXPIYACOC: Veo el llano, el cuerpo desnudo de la tierra, drying beneath the sky.

CUCUMATZ: We name her "Uleu," Madre Tierra.

IXMUCANE: I see rivers like a thousand knives sculpting cañón y arroyo.

IXPIYACOC: I see mountains emerge beneath the parting clouds . . .

CUCUMATZ: And el león y el tigre, el venado, y la culebra will serve as guardians of the earth.

IXMUCANE: And the animals will multiply and make home in branch and bush, in cave and riverbank.

CUCUMATZ: And they will praise their creators . . .

[They are suddenly interrupted by a cacophony of animal sounds.]

CUCUMATZ: What is that?

IXMUCANE: I fear it is the animals, Culebra Verde.

CUCUMATZ: *(Shouting out at the animals)* Stop that ruckus at once! Do you hear me?

IXPIYACOC: We are your father!

IXMUCANE: And we are your mother!

CUCUMATZ: Speak now in a manner befitting of us.

IXPIYACOC: ¿Qué valen estos animales?

IXMUCANE: Son brutos.

CUCUMATZ: ¡Silencio! *(There is sudden silence.)* I hunger for echo of my name, but these creatures speak no godly language. *(Raising up his wings in a fury.)* I banish you ingrates to the caves of night and to the forests dense and dark. From this day forward, you shall be preyed upon and serve as the food for both animal and man!

IXPIYACOC: *(After a pause)* Huracan. . . ?

CUCUMATZ: *(Annoyed)* What is it, Grandfather!

IXPIYACOC: You mentioned . . . food. I'm a little . . . hungry?

CUCUMATZ: *(Half-heartedly)* Let there be Maíz.

[A sack of corn appears at the opening of the pyramid.]

IXPIYACOC: *(Examining it)* ¿Qué es esto? *(He passes it to IXMUCANE)*

IXMUCANE: It's . . . corn, viejo.

IXPIYACOC: Corn?

IXMUCANE: Sí.

CUCUMATZ: *(Disinterested)* See what you can do with it, comadre.

IXMUCANE: Sí, Bahana.

> [*She crosses with the corn to downstage right. She sets up
> the metate and begins to grind. Music: "Metate." IXPIYACOC
> and CUCUMATZ cross to downstage left.*]

IXPIYACOC: What are we going to do now, Kukulcan?

CUCUMATZ: We need to think.

> [*Suddenly disturbed by the sound of the TWINS at play.*]

HUNAHPU: *(Sportscaster's voice)* And Hunahpu drives the ball through
the deathly ring!

CUCUMATZ: What is that racket?

VUCUB: That'll cost you your head!

IXPIYACOC: Son los chavos.

HUNAHPU: But I won!

VUCUB: The winners always get sacrificed.

IXPIYACOC: They sure love that fútbol.

VUCUB: Not by my rules!

CUCUMATZ: Well, it doesn't bode well for their longevity.

> [*The TWINS enter, taunting each other.*]

HUNAHPU: ¡Te hice cachitos! ¡Te hice cachitos!

VUCUB: I'll get you next time!

XMUCANE: ¡Muchachos!

HUNAHPU: We'll see!

IXMUCANE: ¡Ya, paren! ¡Ya paren! Go play en la plazuela. El Señor Culebra y su padre are planning to create the first humans.

VUCUB: Hew mans?

IXMUCANE: Váyanse. They're losing their concentration.

HUNAHPU: Can't we watch?

CUCUMATZ: No! *(To IXPIYACOC)* Vámonos. We won't get a thing done here! *(The GODS exit.)*

IXMUCANE: Ya ven.

VUCUB: *(To HUNAHPU)* C'mon. Rematch.

HUNAHPU: You're on. *(To IXMUCANE, as THE TWINS ascend the pyramid.)* ¡Ay te watcho, jefita!

IXPIYACOC: *(Starts to respond chola-style.)* Ay . . . *(Stops.)* No hablas así. *(To herself)* I don't know where they pick up that barrio slang.

[IXMUCANE exits.]

Scene Three

[The TWINS are playing ball centerstage. TECOLOTE, THE OWL MESSENGER (a four-faced figure) observes the boys from a distance. Music: "Tecolote"; it is a wordless melody, more a cry of warning than a song. A Quiché chant can also be heard from offstage. "Ch'abi Tukur, Hu r A qan Tukur, Kaqix Tukur, Holom Tukur."]

[TECOLOTE descends the pyramid.]

TECOLOTE: *(With authority)* I surmise you are ballplayers.

VUCUB: *(Nervously)* Yes . . . m'am.

HUNAHPU: *(Overlapping)* That's . . . right.

TECOLOTE: Then you are who I've come for.

HUNAHPU: You've come for us?

TECOLOTE: I have.

VUCUB: Forgive us, m'am, but . . . who are you?

TECOLOTE: *(Indignant)* I am Shooting Owl, One-legged Owl, Macaw Owl, and Skull Owl. Otherwise addressed as Tecolote. I am the messenger to the Lords of Death, from the land of Xibalba. *(Chant in the background: "U zamahel Xibalba.")*

THE TWINS: *(In unison)*: Xibalba!

TECOLOTE: Yes. You have the distinct honor of being summoned by the Lords to a match.

HUNAHPU: A ballgame!

TECOLOTE: A ballgame of significant proportion. A match with the very masters of the sport!

VUCUB: But why . . . us?

TECOLOTE: The Lords were duly impressed by the banter of your ball up here.

HUNAHPU: They could hear it?

TECOLOTE: It was impossible not to. All the dust you two were stirring up brought down a rain of mud and thunder in the underworld.

HUNAHPU: They were impressed, you say?

TECOLOTE: Well, let's say they were *interested*. And I'll say no more, except that I will be back to retrieve you at nightfall. *(He raises his stubby neck in a gesture to take flight.)*

VUCUB: You're leaving?

TECOLOTE: I'll meet you at the darkest hour of the night.

VUCUB: How will we see, traveling at that hour?

TECOLOTE: *(Bugging out his eyes)* Four pairs of owl eyes should suffice, I think, to illuminate the dark and foreboding paths that lead to Xibalba.

[*Music: "Tecolote" rises. The OWL takes flight and is gone.*]

VUCUB: She's . . . awesome!

HUNAHPU: Yeah. *(Beat)* This is gonna be great! A real game! No more of this kid's pretend-stuff!

VUCUB: I don't know, Hun, I hear those güeros are a ghostly color down there. Pale people with all the blood sucked out of 'em. That's probably why they want us . . . for fresh blood.

HUNAHPU: They're thirsty for blood and we're thirsty for a good challenge. Anyway, they ain't all pasties down there. Papá told me stories of how some of the women are a beautiful blood red color.

VUCUB: Really.

HUNAHPU: Like the mountains at sunset.

VUCUB: Wow!

HUNAHPU: He said to see such beauty makes you blush red, yourself, from head to toe. *(Beat)* Mira, here comes Mamá. Let's tell her of our journey.

[*IXMUCANE enters with a stack of tortillas.*]

IXMUCANE: ¿Tienes hambre, muchachos? I've got some fresh tortillas for you both!

VUCUB: Tortillas?

HUNAHPU: What's that?

IXMUCANE: Corn cakes.

VUCUB: *(Munching on one)* They're good.

HUNAHPU: *(Taking a bite)* Yeah, but we'll have to take 'em to go, Abuela. We're off to Xibalba to face the Lords of Death.

VUCUB: In a ballgame! *(They start to exit.)*

IXMUCANE: My sons. Espérense. *(They stop.)* Xibalba es una jornada we all must take, but it is not as simple as you think. Los Señores del Infierno are full of trickery and deceit. Cuídanse, hijos. Trust your brain, not your brawn.

VUCUB: No te preocupes, Madre. We'll return . . .

HUNAHPU: ¡Y como campeones!

IXMUCANE: Oye, La Muerte is not so easy to defeat. ¡Que los dioses los bendigan! *(She blesses them as they take their leave.)* In the name of el Tiox, los mundos, y Nantat . . .

Scene Four

[They exit. It is night. The TWINS are met by TECOLOTE who leads them through the pyramid path to the underworld of Xibalba. Underwater sound effects and lighting.]

IXMUCANE: *(Percussion accompaniment)*
Con Tecolote como guía, Vucub y Hunahpu navigate the watery roads of Xibalba.
The rivers run silver with spikes, but my sons are not pierced.
And though thirsty, put neither lip nor tongue to the pus-filled waters.

At the crossroads, all colors converge: el colorado, el negro, el amarillo
  y el blanco.
Pero encontrarán su destino on that blood-black road of Xibalba.
The land of the mirror people of pale and sickly reflection.

*[HUNAHPU and VUCUB complete their journey through the
pyramid, arrive in Xibalba. Lighting transiton to create the dark
world of the infierno. Music: "Xibalba."]*

HUNAHPU: They sure don't make it easy getting here.

VUCUB: This place gives me the creeps. Hey! Where'd Tecolote go?

HUNAHPU: He disappeared. I think we're all on our own here.

*[The Manikins posing as the LORDS OF DEATH stand awkwardly
in the distance. THE TWINS approach.]*

VUCUB: *(Whispering)* Hun, look. I think there are the Lords.

HUNAHPU: *(Extending his hand to the Manikin)* Buenas noches, Señor
  Muerte.

VUCUB: *(Also extending his hand)* Hello, Sir. *(Softly)* God! They look
  really sick!

[The LORDS OF DEATH emerge from their hiding place.]

LORDS OF DEATH: We are sick!

*[The TWINS grab each other. THE LORDS OF DEATH bust up
into vile and insidious laughter.]*

PATRIARCHAL PUS: Fools! We are the real Lords of Death!

LORDS OF DEATH:
  We are spilled blood and broken bones.
  We are hemorrhage and cancer of the marrow.
  We are vomited guts and infected wounds,
  we drink pus and blood and like it!
  Sudden deaths in subway stations,
  a quick blade to the heart!

The slow dissolution of body and bone
by a hunger left in the dark.

Name the disease, we invented it!
And we daily dream up more!
Silent plagues are our favorite,
a game of cellular war.

This is the home of Cizin
who passes a gruesome gas.
No one escapes our odor
nor the call of the water-lilied path.

PATRIARCHAL PUS: You boys must be weary after your long journey; take the load off your feet. *(Indicating the "hot seat.")*

HUNAHPU: Thanks.

VUCUB: Yeah.

[They both sit down at once, scorching their butts.]

THE TWINS: ¡Ay, Carajo! Ouch! My nalgas!

[The heat of the seat tosses them onto the ground. The LORDS OF DEATH again are thoroughly delighted and are laughing uproariously.]

BLOOD SAUSAGE: I hope you two haven't thoroughly ruined your backsides.

HUNAHPU: *(Holding his wounded butt, under his breath)* We'll still kick your butts tomorrow.

BLOOD SAUSAGE: That's the spirit. Now, we must make sure that you're well rested for the Big Game.

[THE LORDS OF DEATH escort THE TWINS to a small hutch-like cell where they are to spend the night.]

PATRIARCHAL PUS: Welcome to La Posada, our South of the Border Theme House. You should find it *(mispronouncing)* co-MO-da. Good night, gentlemen.

BLOOD SAUSAGE: And . . . good luck.

[They lock them in.]

PATRIARCHAL PUS: Why wait? We should just be rid of them tonight. A human sacrifice would be equally as entertaining as any ballgame.

BLOOD SAUSAGE: Yes! *(Calling out)* Owl! The Instrument of Sacrifice! At once!

TECOLOTE: Sacrifice . . . ?

PATRIARCHAL PUS: Are you deaf, Owl? Have the gods given you those big ears for nothing?

TECOLOTE: No sir, I mean, yessir! *(He exits.)*

BLOOD SAUSAGE: These young athletic types bring such pleasure to a sacrifice.

PATRIARCHAL PUS: Yes, all those red corpuscles just pumping with life!

[TECOLOTE returns with the obsidian blade.]

PATRIARCHAL PUS: Ah! The obsidian blade!

TECOLOTE: *(Anxiously)* Will you be needing my services any more this morning, sirs?

BLOOD SAUSAGE: What's the rush, Owl?

TECOLOTE: No rush, your Lordship. It's merely that I'm feeling a little . . . under the weather.

BLOOD SAUSAGE: You offend me, Owl, with your complaints.

TECOLOTE: Yes . . . sir.

PATRIARCHAL PUS: Brother, you can do the honors! *(Handing him the obsidian blade.)*

BLOOD SAUSAGE: Most generous of you, Pat Pus.

PATRIARCHAL PUS: Owl, announce to the boys that the sun has risen.

TECOLOTE: Right away, your Lordship.

[TECOLOTE crosses to the cell, knocks on the door. BLOOD SAUSAGE hovers next to the owl, the blade poised in the air.]

TECOLOTE: Hunahpu! Vucub! Come, look out at the sky. The sun is rising. It is a beautiful blood red morning!

[As the TWINS stick out their heads to look, BLOOD SAUSAGE decapitates them. The heads fly into the air. THE LORDS catch them and salivate over them.

PATRARCHAL PUS: Owl, here, put the elder brother's head into that old dried-up tree. No harm in giving the Xibalbans a little reminder—

BLOOD SAUSAGE: Of the price of defiance.

[TECOLOTE places HUNAHPU's head into the calabash tree which rises from the center of the pyramid.]

Scene Five

[Lighting transition. Music: "Fertility." The once-barren tree gradually blossoms into a calabash tree, heavily laden with fruit. HUNAHPU's head sits in it.]

HUNAHPU: *(To himself, bitterly)* All of Xibalba will be talking about how gorgeous this old tree is, now that my head's stuck into it. I wonder what they did with Vucub's head. Probably using it for a fútbol. Yep, fruit abounds now all around me. Calabash for days! *(Ixquic enters.)* Who is this? ¡Qué belleza! She is exactly as Papá described her, el color de los antiplanos cuando se pone el sol. But she seems so sad. I must speak to her. *(IXQUIC approaches the calabash tree.)*

IXQUIC: *(Canto)*
> Antes era un arbol seco
> ahora estás lleno de vida.
> Your branches me quieren acariciar,
> and your leaves tiemblan
> cuando paso por acá.
>
> ¿Por qué me tormentas así?
> ¿Por qué me invitas
> a bailar con tus hojas en la brisa.
> abrazar tus ramas fuertes,
> hold your sweet fruit in my eager palm?
>
> Te tengo que probar.
> Hasta en mis sueños
> te puedo saborear.
>
> *(Spoken)* Must I die of this relentless hunger?

HUNAHPU: No.

IXQUIC: Who speaks?

HUNAHPU: It's me. La calavera, I mean the calabash, I mean the jícara, I mean here in the tree. See my moving mouth.

IXQUIC: Are you the devil?

HUNAHPU: No your Daddy's the devil, he's the one who got me into this gourd.

IXQUIC: I don't think you should talk about my father.

HUNAHPU: I'm sorry.

IXQUIC: *(Pause)* What were you going to say to me?

HUNAHPU: I said, Ixquic, you shouldn't die of hunger.

IXQUIC: How do you know my name?

HUNAHPU: By your color. My father told me . . . he was right. You *are* a beautiful earth color, Blood Woman.

IXQUIC: Too dark.

HUNAHPU: No, why do you say that?

IXQUIC: Here in Xibalba . . . with the blood-less Lords. They want everyone empty and bone-gray like them.

HUNAHPU: Come to my country. There the Blue-Green Kukulcan reigns. And Ixmucane and Ixpiyacoc, my parents, they love all their children.

IXQUIC: You tempt me. You do look delicious.

HUNAHPU: I am. Would you like a little sample?

IXQUIC: Yes.

HUNAHPU: Then extend your right hand.

IXQUIC: You won't harm me?

HUNAHPU: I will only give you a taste of the life you seek.

[*She extends her hand, he spits into it.*]

IXQUIC: But it's nothing but a chisguete.

HUNAHPU: That little spit will bear the sweetest fruit. It is the liquid life of our descendants that shall be born again in our children.

IXQUIC: I am to be their mother?

HUNAHPU: Yes. Through them we shall not perish. Now hurry! Súbete a la tierra.

[*IXQUIC hurries away. She presses the palm of spit to her breast, and she immediately blossoms, her blood red color deepening. Lighting transiton. Music: "Fertility." The LORDS OF DEATH enter.*]

PATRIARCHAL PUS: Do you smell something foul, Blood Sausage?

BLOOD SAUSAGE: Yes, there is a stench in the air . . .

PATRIARCHAL PUS: *(Upon the sight of IXQUIC pregnant)* It is you! You have deceived me! You have dishonored our name! You are a traitoress and a slut!

IXQUIC: But Father, I have not known a man in the biblical sense.

PATRIARCHAL PUS: This is not the bible. This is the *Popol Vuh*. *(Thunderous)* Who is responsible for this crime?

IXQUIC: The crime of life?

PATRIARCHAL PUS: The crime of that swell in your belly.

BLOOD SAUSAGE: What a rotten smell!

IXQUIC: With all due respect, your honor, it's motherhood.

PATRIARCHAL PUS: It's female wantonness!

IXQUIC: It's fertility. But what would you old men know of that.

BLOOD SAUSAGE: What insolence! She must die! *(To PATRIARCHAL PUS)* You are in accord, Brother Lord?

PATRIARCHAL PUS *(Eyeing IXQUIC with utter contempt)* So be it! *(Calling out)* Owl!

TECOLOTE: *(Entering)* My Lord?

PATRIARCHAL PUS: Cut her heart out and bring it to us in a jícara gourd.

IXQUIC: Father?

PATRIARCHAL PUS: I have no daughter. *(To OWL)* Take her away at once. The sight of her pregnant with so much life revolts me!

TECOLOTE: *(Sadly)* Come with me, Blood woman.

[*TECOLOTE reluctantly starts to drag IXQUIC away, as the LORDS OF DEATH exit.*]

IXQUIC: No, wait. *(TECOLOTE stops.)* Betray your master, wise Owl. What I carry in my womb germinated of its own choosing as I contemplated the sudden beauty of the calabash tree. This living heart that beats next to mine is a gift from the gods. How can we refuse their generosity?

TECOLOTE: But what am I to do about your heart, Ixquic? The Lords will surely have my head were I to return without it.

IXQUIC: My heart will stay inside my breast. My breast will spill no blood, only sweet milky sap for my growing sons. Give me the filero, Teco. *(TECOLOTE does. IXQUIC goes to the tree.)* And a gourd. *(TECOLOTE follows with a gourd. IXQUIC drives the blade into the breast of the tree.)* La leche de madre . . . as fragrant as the sap that bleeds from this tree. *(The sap spills out.)* Now gather this copal into this jícara and present it to my cruel father and his brother of Death. It will burn and curdle like my own dark blood.

[*TECOLOTE puts a gourd below the mouth of the wound to catch the bleeding sap.*]

TECOLOTE: *(Holding the gourd between them)* Blood Woman, you must escape this hell. You have too much life for this place.

IXQUIC: Teco.

TECOLOTE: You were never meant to live beneath the Lords' ghostly shadow. *(IXQUIC wraps her hands around TECOLOTE's.)*

IXQUIC: Dear Tecolote, I swear by my sons' divine origins, you too shall be freed from this place. You shall inherit the bright face of Uleu and reside upon the earth's generous countenance.

[*IXQUIC rushes off. The LORDS OF DEATH enter.*]

BLOOD SAUSAGE: Well, brother, it appears by the eager look of our messenger, that her task has been well executed!

PATRIARCHAL PUS: Indeed. What's that you hold trembling inside your feathered grip, Owl Messenger?

TECOLOTE: It is the heart of your deceitful daughter, your lordship, as you requested.

BLOOD SAUSAGE: *(Rubbing his hands together, salivating)* Ah!

PATRIARCHAL PUS: Bring it here! *(TECOLOTE presents the gourd to the LORDS. PAT PUS dips his fingers into the gourd.)* Oh yes, this has the look and feel of an unfaithful heart! Don't you think, Brother?

BLOOD SAUSAGE: *(Digging his fingers into the gourd)* Delicious!

PATRIARCHAL PUS: What a marvelous fragrance!

BLOOD SAUSAGE: There is nothing sweeter!

[*The LORDS OF DEATH exit with the gourd, following the intoxicating scent off the stage. TECOLOTE remains alone on stage.*]

TECOLOTE: What have I done? I have deceived the Lords! I've saved Blood Woman's life and . . . my own, I think. She promises freedom, la tierra as home. Uleu, . . . I'm trembling. Receive me, madre.

[*Fade out.*]

Scene Six

[*IXQUIC stands at the top of the pyramid path.*]

IXQUIC: *(Canto, journeying)*
Without father or husband, without mother or guide,
I enter la tierra sagrada, orphaned of home and history.

The twin beating of my babies' breath is the only company I keep.
How will they receive me in this land of celestial strangers?

Will they blame me for the wickedness of my father?
. . . my delight at the taste of calabash, spilling from a once-barren tree?

[Downstage right, IXMUCANE is grinding away at her metate, periodically wiping her eyes. The tears mix with the masa as she grinds. IXQUIC approaches timidly.]

IXQUIC: Señora . . . ? Madre . . . ?

IXMUCANE: Who calls me mother?

IXQUIC: Soy tu nuera.

IXMUCANE: I have no daughter-in-law, no children. My last born have died in Xibalba. Don't you see how my tears salt the masa of these tortillas? Why do you come here and aggravate me?

IXQUIC: No la quiero molestar. But your herencia lives inside me y cuando doy a luz you will recognize in my children's faces the features of the sons you mourn.

IXMUCANE: Impostor!

IXQUIC: And if I'm not. . . ?

[IXMUCANE studies IXQUIC for a moment.]

IXMUCANE: Bueno . . . *(She rises slowly, wipes her hands on her apron.)* I will have to see for myself.

IXQUIC: Test me as you must, Señora. I know who I am and I bring you no falsehoods.

IXMUCANE: Enough said. Ven conmigo. *(She gives IXQUIC a net for harvesting.)* If you are so sure that you are my daughter, then start behaving like one.

[They go to the milpa. It is a barren field with one lone corn plant withering at its center.]

IXMUCANE: Aquí está mi milpa. Tapizca this net of maíz and return it full to me.

IXQUIC: As you wish. *(She starts to exit.)*

IXMUCANE: Full, te digo. And don't deplete my field.

IXQUIC: Sí, Señora.

[IXMUCANE exits.]

IXQUIC: But this is not a test. It is a trick! How am I to fill this net from such barren ground? *(Looking up to the moon)* Querida Diosa Ixchel, Guardia del Bastimiento, te pido tu ayuda. *(She begins to chant, praying to the four directions.)*

>
> ucah tzucuxic
> ucah xucutaxic
>   retaxic,
> ucah cheexic,
>
> umeh camaxic,
> uyuc camaxic
>
> upa cah,
> upa uleu
>
> cah tzuc
> cah xucut

[Suddenly the figure of la diosa de maíz appears at the pyramid's peak. Corn spills forth from her mouth.]

IXQUIC: X Toh, X Q'anil, X Kakav! Las Diosas have answered my prayers!

IXMUCANE: *(Entering)* It will soon be dawn and I have received no . . . *(Seeing the mountain of corn)* ¡Hija bendita! El dios de maíz te ha tocado. *(She embraces her.)* Daughter of corn and light! ¡Basta! ¡De verdad, eres mi hija! Ayúdame, mija. *(She begins stuffing the corn into the net.)* Mi viejo will be thrilled to see que abundancia le trae su nuera a la familia. Con tanto corn, we will surely be busy con la tamalada tonight!

IXQUIC: *(Holding her womb)* Mother-dearest, I think la tamalada will have to wait. The twins announce their entrance.

IXMUCANE: ¿Cómo? *(Noticing that IXQUIC is going into labor.)* Mijita! ¿Estás dando a luz?

IXQUIC: *(In a panic)* Sí. Ahorita!

IXMUCANE: ¡Ay, te ayudo! *(She goes to her.)*

IXQUIC: *(Nervously)* ¿Eres partera?

IXMUCANE: ¿Qué crees? These hands have caught thousands of celestial beings. Now cállese y push! *(IXQUIC goes into labor, rising before the pyramid. IXMUCANE chants:)*

Xa ta'jun hora o media hora
cuya ri luz, cuya ri sak.

[*IXQUIC gives birth to IXBALANQUE and HUNAHPU. They come somersaulting out from beneath her long skirt.*]

IXMUCANE: *(Naming each twin as he emerges)* K alaxik Hun Ah Pu X Balan ke!

[*At first they are infants, sucking their thumbs and cuddling up to their mother and grandmother. They emit infant sounds, gurgling playfully. Then they begin to walk, trying out their first shaky steps as toddlers. HUNAHPU, the more aggressive one, tries first, then his brother follows suit. They fall on their butts numerous times until they get the hang of it. This may be performed as a kind of dance piece between LOS GEMELOS and assisted by IXMUCANE and IXQUIC. Verbal exclamations are made throughout, until finally LOS GEMELOS are noticeably full grown. HUNAHPU finds some corn and begins trying to juggle it in the air. IXBALANQUE joins him, tossing the corn back and forth. THE WOMEN observe.*]

HUNAHPU: Mira mamá! What do you think of this?

IXQUIC: That's nice, hijo! *(To IXMUCANE)* I fear Hunahpu may have inherited his father's love of sports.

IXMUCANE: Es el destino, daughter.

IXQUIC: Pero, ves al otro. *(Referring to IXBALANQUE)* He's not quite as adept.

IXMUCANE: But a ballplayer nonetheless. I would have hoped for at least one scribe in the family!

IXQUIC: He does look intelligent.

IXMUCANE: Ni modo. Whatever they turn out to be, they must first learn the lesson of hard work.

IXQUIC: Verdad.

IXMUCANE: *(Calling out to them)* Come here, my sweet-boys, your mother has something to tell you. *(They go to her.)*

IXBALANQUE: ¿Mande, Señora?

HUNAHPU: ¿Sí, mamá?

IXQUIC: This field is ready for replanting. Treat the earth well and she will reward you with abundance and long-life. Here are your planting sticks. *(She hands the sticks to LOS GEMELOS.)*

HUNAHPU: Planting sticks. . . ?

IXMUCANE: Your tools. Váyanse.

[The women exit. LOS GEMELOS cross to the empty field and stare at it in bewilderment.]

HUNAHPU: And we were just getting warmed up.

IXBALANQUE: I know.

HUNAHPU: This dirt doesn't look like it can produce much of anything.

IXBALANQUE: Really.

[*Begrudgingly, IXBALANQUE and HUNAHPU start digging the ground and planting seed.*]

IXBALANQUE: I don't see the reward in it. I feel like we're just wasting our time.

HUNAHPU: Well, Abuela sees it differently. *(Imitating her)* "First they must learn the lesson of hard work."

IXBALANQUE: Truth is 'mano. I think what Abuela really sees, she ain't tellin' us.

HUNAHPU: What d'ya mean?

IXBALANQUE: I don't know. It's just a feeling.

[*HUNAHPU leans on his stick thinking on this.*]

IXBALANQUE: C'mon, Hun.

HUNAHPU: . . . All right.

[*They return to work. Their efforts are obviously half-hearted. Suddenly they hit upon a lump in the ground.*]

RAT: Jesus H. Christ!

VUCUB: Who? Whadya say, Hun?

HUNAHPU: I didn't say anything.

[*They continue working.*]

RAT: Hey! *(Rat pops up out of the ground.)* Watch where you're pokin' that stick.

HUNAHPU: It's a rat! Grab it!

[*Music/percussion. They grab the rat, tossing it back and forth. It screams out.*]

RAT: Get ya friggin' paws offa me! Put me down! Put me down, ya buncha babies. Stop! What would your ole man think of yous, pickin' on somebody ain't half your size. *(They stop.)*

IXBALANQUE: You know our father?

RAT: You'd think I'd lie about a thing like that . . . ? 'Bout a person's flesh 'n' blood?

IXBALANQUE: Well, no, but . . .

HUNAHPU: Ah, he's bluffing. Give me him!

[HUNAHPU grabs the RAT out of IXBALANQUE's hands.]

RAT: Put me down, punk, or I ain't tellin' you jack.

IXBALANQUE: Put him down, Hun.

HUNAHPU: *(Setting RAT down)* So, tell us.

RAT: Cheezus! What your ole lady put in your corn cakes this morning?

HUNAHPU: Quit stalling.

IXBALANQUE: What do you know about our father?

RAT: I know he'd be purty broken up to find you stooped over some lump of dirt with a hoe in your hand. *(There is a pause.)*

HUNAHPU: That's it? That's all you have to say?

RAT: You're ball players, dummies. Don't you get it? Jus' like your ole man and his brutha and his ole man . . . etcetera, etcetera, etcetera.

HUNAHPU: Abuelo, too?

RAT: Well, he don't play no more. He's old.

IXBALANQUE: Yeah, but . . . what's a ball player?

RAT: *(Somewhat exasperated)* It's freedom! Prestige! Honor! And it sure beats bustin' your butt out here in the fields.

HUNAHPU: Sounds like our kind of game!

RAT: Yeah, but it can get a little messy at times . . .

IXBALANQUE: Messy?

RAT: Well . . . a little . . . bloody. But you don't have to lose your head over it. C'mon, I know where the ball equipment is stored. Yokes, hand stones, hachas, the works! Every jock's dream come true.

IXBALANQUE: *(To himself)* Jock?

HUNAHPU: *(To IXBALANQUE)* Are you game?

IBALANQUE: *(Hesitating for moment, then)* Yeah, let's go! Which way, Rat?

RAT: That-a-way. *(The GEMELOS start to exit.)* Hey! Take me with yous!

[They grab the RAT and all exit excitedly. Fade out.]

Scene Seven

[Lighting transition. Music: "The World of the Gods." THE GODS reconvene. IXPIYACOC is molding mud into a human-like form. CUCUMATZ hovers over him, whispering directives. IXMUCANE and IXQUIC enter.]

IXMUCANE: Ahora que we finally got the boys to work, we can return a nuestros quehaceres.

IXQUIC: *(Indicating her embroidery)* Verdad. Esta huipil me estaba llamando. The dream goes dim, it's time to finish it.

IXMUCANE: Pues, sí. Ya es hora. And I got a house full of men to feed.

[IXMUCANE begins turning tortillas on the comal. IXQUIC returns to her embroidery. They work in silence as the gods continue shaping the mud-man.]

CUCUMATZ: *(After a pause)* I think we're close to making something human here.

IXMUCANE: *(Overhearing)* ¿De verdad? ¿Qué tienes? *(IXMUCANE crosses to where IXPIYACOC is working.)*

IXPIYACOC: It's a mud-person.

IXMUCANE: A mud-person, but I don't think . . .

CUCUMATZ: *(Totally engrossed, to IXPIYACOC)* Add a flatter forehead and a broader nose.

IXPIYACOC: How's that?

CUCUMATZ: Mejor.

IXMUCANE: Pero un cuerpo de barro no servirá de na . . .

IXPIYACOC: *(Ignoring her)* ¡Eso! Terminamos. All that is required is your breath of life, Cucumatz.

[CUCUMATZ leans over and breathes into the being.]

IXPIYACOC: Now, speak up little one. Sing praises to your creator. *(They wait, no response.)* Speak up, I say! *(Again, no response.)*

CUCUMATZ: *(Worried)* He can't hear you.

IXPIYACOC: Tal vez está sordo!

IXMUCANE: Te dije.

CUCUMATZ: Possibly I made some error in calculation . . . an improper balance of elements.

[IXMUCANE picks up a small pitcher of water and pours it over the mud-man.]

IXPIYACOC: ¿Qué 'stás haciendo, mujer?

CUCUMATZ: Have you gone mad?

IXMUCANE: With all due respect, compadre, that was your first
spring rains.

IXPIYACOC: It's collapsed!

IXMUCANE: *(Nonchalant)* Qué pena. *(IXMUCANE returns to the comal.
To IXQUIC as she passes.)* Pictures speak louder than words.
(IXQUIC smiles.)

CUCUMATZ: *(Noticeably disturbed)* She's right. This mud-man isn't strong
enough to weather even one highland season.

IXPIYACOC: What shall we do now, Culebra Sabia?

CUCUMATZ: We'll have to try something else. *(Pause)* Let's see . . .
I know! We shall start with the finest grain of wood from the ceiba
tree. *(They are interrupted by the sound of ball playing.)*

IXBALANQUE: Kick it, Hun!

IXMUCANE: *(Under her breath)* Oh no, not again.

HUNAHPU: What a shot!

CUCUMATZ: It's a miracle we get anything done around this place.

[*LOS GEMELOS' banter continues.*]

IXQUIC: I'm sorry, Don Culebra.

IXMUCANE: *(To herself)* And I had hidden the playing equipment so well.

IXPIYACOC: *(To IXQUIC)* Tell the boys they disturb their godfathers.

IXQUIC: Sí, señor.

[*IXQUIC exits.*]

IXMUCANE: *(To herself)* ¡Qué arrogancia! . . . to think I could defy destiny.

CUCUMATZ: *(To IXPIYACOC who holds the ceiba wood)* Now the first penetrations into the head are very important. Follow the grain of the wood exactly.

IXPIYACOC: Yes, Cucumatz. *(He begins to carve the wood.)*

CUCUMATZ: That's right.

[LOS GEMELOS enter with ball.]

IXBALANQUE: Sorry about the noise, Godfathers . . .

HUNAHPU: *(Spying the creation.)* Hey, what are you making?

CUCUMATZ: The human race, my sons.

IXBALANQUE: What's a human race?

HUNAHPU: Can we join?

CUCUMATZ: Certainly not. You are gods.

HUNAHPU: Why can't gods be in the race?

IXPIYACOC: It's not a contest. It's a . . . people.

HUNAHPU: *(Not understanding)* Oh.

IXBALANQUE: What's a . . . people?

CUCUMATZ: Living beings who long to know the face of their creator.

IXPIYACOC: Run along now. We'll let you know when we're finished.

IXBALANQUE: Promise?

CUCUMATZ: ¡Váyanse, ya!

IXPIYACOC: Go to the plazuela to play.

HUNAHPU: Yes sirs!

> [*LOS GEMELOS exit toward la plazuela. CUCUMATZ and IXPIYACOC return to work. IXQUIC goes to IXMUCANE who is noticeably disturbed, grinding her distress into the corn.*]

IXQUIC: Mamá, is there something you wish to tell me?

IXMUCANE: *(Grinding)* No.

IXQUIC: At times, my sons act as strangers. I fear they are leaving me.

IXMUCANE: It's natural.

IXQUIC: The fear? Or their leaving?

IXMUCANE: Both. Both are as common as this corn.

> [*CUCUMATZ and IXPIYACOC finish the final touches of a wooden sculpture of a human. It is doll-sized and Maya in features.*]

IXPIYACOC: Cucumatz, it's gorgeous. We have truly created a thing of beauty.

CUCUMATZ: *(Putting away their sculpting tools.)* Se ve bien, ¿no?

IXPIYACOC: Muy bien.

CUCUMATZ: It bears intelligence in its look.

IXPIYACOC: But can it speak?

CUCUMATZ: So be it.

WOODEN-MAN: I'm hungry.

CUCUMATZ: These are the first words of our divine creation?

> [*CUCUMATZ, clearly disturbed, rethinks the problem. He reviews his steps to himself as the action continues.*]

CUCUMATZ: But the ceiba was strong and well-aged . . .

WOODEN-MAN: Do you hear me? I'm starving!

CUCUMATZ: We used the sharpest of obsidian edges to imbue the head with clarity and self-reflection . . .

WOODEN-MAN: *(Overlapping)* Tengo mucho hambre!

IXPIYACOC: *(Calling out)* Vieja!

IXMUCANE: Sí, corazón.

IXPIYACOC: Feed this stick-man something. He complains of hunger.

CUCUMATZ: What could I have forgotten? The wood was thoroughly sanded, which should have resulted in a soft-spoken being with a mild manner.

WOODEN-MAN: ¡Quiero comer!

CUCUMATZ: Feed him, please. I grow impatient to know if he can express something beyond animal needs.

IXMUCANE: Allí voy.

WOODEN-MAN: Give me something to eat!

IXMUCANE: Allí voy. Allí voy. *(She brings him two pots of food.)* He *is* a nice-looking fellow.

WOODEN-MAN: *(To IXMUCANE, copping a feel)* ¡Tú también, te ves sabrosa!

IXMUCANE: ¡Qué grosero!

CUCUMATZ: He's obscene!

[*WOODEN-MAN devours the food, banging the pots around.*]

IXPIYACOC: Hardly godly in his manners!

WOODEN-MAN: *(Banging)* I want more!

[In moments, the pots begin to complain.]

OLLAS: Hey! Handle me with care!
    Stop beating me, I'm fragile.
    Yeah, we're just made of clay!
    Watch it! You're spilling my guts!

WOODEN-MAN: Give me some more food!

[The GODS watch in horror as the WOODEN-MAN eats raven-ously, without notice of his creators or the complaints of the kitchen utensils. The pots rebel, begin to attack the WOODEN-MAN.]

OLLAS: Take that, you callous thug!
    Pot-oppressor!
    Bowl Abuser!
    We'll pound you down to sawdust!

[They beat the WOODEN-MAN until he falls to the ground.]

IXPIYACOC: Well, it was just an experiment.

CUCUMATZ: A failed one.

[IXPIYACOC picks up the broken man from the ground and the GODS exit, mumbling to themselves.]

CUCUMATZ: We didn't even get a word of thanks.

IXPIYACOC: A song of praise! A postcard!

[Crossfade to IXMUCANE who is grinding corn at the metate. IXQUIC is embroidering.]

IXPIYACOC: The wooden-man had no heart.

IXQUIC: Verdad. But he did look human.

IXPIYACOC: So do the monkeys.

[The women laugh, then are suddenly interrupted. Music: "Tecolote." The OWL appears at the top of the pyramid. They watch her as she descends. There is a sense of foreboding in the air.]

IXMUCANE: *(To TECOLOTE)* I imagine you will find who you are looking for, playing ball en la plazuela. *(TECOLOTE exits without a word.)*

IXQUIC: . . . Mother?

IXMUCANE: *(Rises, wipes her hands on her apron)* Ya vámonos, hija. The story is already written.

[IXQUIC accompanies IXMUCANE out to the patio centerstage. IXMUCANE gets down on her knees and pulls out two young corn plants from her apron pocket. She hands one to IXQUIC.]

IXMUCANE: Toma.

IXQUIC: What is this for, Madre?

IXMUCANE: A prayer of life for your sons.

IXQUIC: I don't understand.

IXMUCANE: Siémbrala en la tierra, hija. *(They both plant the corn stalks into the ground.)* And each day as you enter el patio, observe the plants well. Should the plants grow dry and desert gray, Xibalba will be our sons' resting place. But should these plants bear new leaves of green, they shall return to us as sun and moon and light.

[LOS GEMELOS enter.]

IXQUIC: ¡Hijos!

HUNAHPU: Hello, mother.

IXBALANQUE: Beloved grandmother.

IXMUCANE: My sons.

IXBALANQUE: Grandmother, you've already planted the corn. You've known all along, haven't you, la jornada that lays before us?

IXMUCANE: I am not ignorant of fate, as I have already suffered the loss of your father and uncle.

IXQUIC: And now I, too, understand your destiny.

[LOS GEMELOS go to their grandmother and mother. They embrace.]

IXMUCANE: Go now, the Lords of Death await you. *(Blessing them)* In the name of el Tiox, los mundos , y Nantat . . .

[LOS GEMELOS take their leave and travel down the pyramid path to Xibalba. TECOLOTE leads the way, then vanishes. Lighting transition to the underworld. Music: "Xibalba."]

Scene Eight

[THE GEMELOS hide, just as THE LORDS OF DEATH enter. TECOLOTE follows.]

BLOOD SAUSAGE: Did you hear something, Pat Pus?

PATRIARCHAL PUS: We aren't expecting anyone at this hour.

[LOS GEMELOS jump out of hiding.]

HUNAHPU: Good day, Lord Blood Sausage.

BLOOD SAUSAGE: What the bloody hell . . . !

IXB ALANQUE: Señor Patriarchal Pus.

PATRIARCHAL PUS: *(Startled)* You nearly scared us to death!

BLOOD SAUSAGE: How did you know our names?

HUNAHPU: A good guess . . . ?

BLOOD SAUSAGE: Humph! *(Indicating the "hot seat")* Have a seat and give us a moment to think about what to do with you.

HUNAHPU: No, sirs! It is you who have suffered the shock. Take a moment to recoup yourselves.

PATRIARCHAL PUS: He's right.

BLOOD SAUSAGE: Most thoughtful of them.

[The LORDS OF DEATH unwittingly sit on the "hot seat."]

PATRIARCHAL PUS: Ouch!

BLOOD SAUSAGE: Ooooh! My blistered buttocks!

PATRIARCHAL PUS: You busters think you're pretty smart, don't you?

IXBALANQUE: Well sirs, we do know the difference between a comal and a couch.

BLOOD SAUSAGE: All right then, smart alecks . . . *(Calling out)* Owl!

TECOLOTE: Yes, your lordship.

BLOOD SAUSAGE: Put these hooligans in the House of Bats!

PATRIARCHAL PUS: No one survives those nocturnal navigators!

[He escorts LOS GEMELOS to their cell.]

PATRIARCH PUS: *(To BLOOD SAUSAGE as they exit)* I don't know what it is about those boys, they feel so . . . familiar.

TECOLOTE *(Muttering)* DNA.

[TECOLOTE puts LOS GEMELOS in the hutch.]

TECOLOTE: Keep your heads covered.

IXBALANQUE: What?

TECOLOTE: The bats. They got snouts like knives.

IXBALANQUE: . . . Oh.

*[TECOLOTE closes the hutch door. LOS GEMELOS wait for
the bats to arrive. Suddenly a field of moving darkness passes over
the heads of LOS GEMELOS. A bat figure enters and dances
menacingly around the hutch. The sound of beating wings and
a loathsome squeaking fills the air. Then there is silence as the bat
hovers above the boys' cell.]*

IXBALANQUE: *(timidly)* Hun?

HUNAHPU: Yeah.

IXBALANQUE: I think the bats are gone now. Can you see if it's close
to dawn?

HUNAHPU: Okay, I'll go check it out.

IXBALANQUE: Be careful.

*[As HUNAHPU sticks out his head to look for the dawn, the bat flies
by and snatches off HUNAHPU's head, dancing about with it as she
exits.]*

IXBALANQUE: Hun! Hun! *(He pokes his head out.)* What happened?
(Calling out) Tecolote! Tecolote!

TECOLOTE: What's the problem?

IXBALANQUE: It's Hunahpu. He's lost his head.

TECOLOTE: I told you to stay under cover.

[CONEJO enters.]

CONEJO: Oye, carnala ¿qué pasa?

TECOLOTE: Hunahpu's lost his head.

CONEJO: ¿De veras? The bats?

TECOLOTE: I tried to warn them.

CONEJO: Blood-thirsty little cabrones. I guess that was the round thing con cara de dios que was rollin' around in the ball court.

IXB ALANQUE: You saw my brother's head! Can you get it back?

CONEJO: Pues . . . I got an idea. 'Spérete aquí. *(CONEJO disappears.)*

IXB ALANQUE: What's he up to?

TECOLOTE: You'll see.

CONEJO: *(Returning with a large squash)* ¡Toma! *(He tosses the squash to IXBALANQUE.)*

TECOLOTE: Good thinking, Rabbit.

IXBALANQUE: What's the squash for?

CONEJO: Un sub.

IXBALANQUE: A sub?

CONEJO: Un substitute!

IXBALANQUE: I still don't get it.

CONEJO: Vente. *(They huddle close together. TECOLOTE keeps watch.)* Hunahpu's gonna hafta fake it like this squash is his cabeza-head. Otherwise, you forfeit the game.

IXBALANQUE: We can't forfeit!

CONEJO: Por eso, digo you gotta follow my game plan. They'll be using your carnal's real head as the ball today.

IXBALANQUE: Ouch!

CONEJO: No te agüites. He'll survive. *(Continuing)* Half way through the game, I'll whistle and that'll be la señal for you vatos to kick the ball as far out of bounds as you can. En el mismo momento, I'll bounce off like a ball p'alla in a different direction. The Lords son tan pendejos, they'll chase after anything that moves. While they're busy huffin' and puffin' after me, you make the switch.

IXBALANQUE: Oh, now I get it. And I stick Hun's real head back on.

CONEJO: Eso!

IXBALANQUE: And we use the squash for the ball.

CONEJO: Orale! That's the strategy.

IXBALANQUE: Will it work?

CONEJO: Este . . . *(Kisses the air)* Suavecito!

[*IXBALANQUE places the squash on HUNAHPU's head.*]

IXBALANQUE: Try this on, Bro. *(HUNAHPU emerges from hutch wearing squash-head.)* How you feel, melon?

HUNAHPU: *(Muffled)* All right . . . I guess.

IXBALANQUE: *(His ear to the squash)* Yeah, great. Okay, let's go. We got a game to win.

[*They exit.*]

Scene Nine

[*Conch shells announce the day of the Ball Game. LOS GEMELOS enter. They are in full ballgame regalia, The LORDS OF DEATH stand at the top of the pyramid.*]

PATRIARCHAL PUS: Xibalbans! It has been brought to our attention that Hunahpu, the son of his similarly fated father, Hunahpu the First, has generously donated his head for the purposes of today's ballgame!

BLOOD SAUSAGE: A round of applause for the donor!

[THE LORDS OF DEATH descend with the head ceremoniously. The opponents face each other off. For a moment the LORDS appear a bit confused, seeing HUNAHPU standing before them while they hold his head in their hands. But eager for a good game, they proceed. The conch shell again sounds and the ball game begins. Percussion. The ballgame is a kind of death-dealing slow-motion dance.

Suddenly CONEJO lets out a loud whistle and IXBALANQUE kicks the ball off the field. CONEJO runs off in a different direction, pretending to be the ball.]

BLOOD SAUSAGE: There goes the ball!

PATRIARCHAL PUS: Let's get it!

[THE LORDS OF DEATH chase after CONEJO. In the meantime, HUNAHPU grabs the real ball (HUNAHPU's head) and replaces the squash with it. The squash now becomes the ball. They rush back into the center of the court.]

IXBALANQUE: We've retrieved it! We've got the ball over here!

PATRIARCHAL PUS: But I don't understand. Didn't the ball roll over there?

BLOOD SAUSAGE: Who cares? Let's get back to the game!

[THE LORDS OF DEATH return to the ballgame, a bit disoriented. The ballgame ensues. HUNAHPU kicks the ball and hits the goal-ring at the top of the pyramid. The squash-ball splits in two.]

HUNAHPU: Our game! We won! We won!

[LOS GEMELOS win the game. THE LORDS OF DEATH exit in disgust.]

BLOOD SAUSAGE: This is an outrage!

PATRIARCHAL PUS: If word should get out . . . that these pubescents defeated us . . . with a squash!

BLOOD SAUSAGE: Well, their victory will be short-lived. I assure you.

Scene Ten

[After the ballgame, LOS GEMELOS sit up on the pyramid.]

HUNAHPU: We won, so why don't I feel good?

IXBALANQUE: Cuz that's not the point.

HUNAHPU: What . . . ? Feeling good?

IXBALANQUE: No, winning.

HUNAHPU: But winning's everything, Ix.

IXBALANQUE: Maybe when we were kids, but not now. *(Sniffing the air)* Smell that?

HUNAHPU: What? *(Sniffing)* It's . . . barbeque.

IXBALANQUE: It's us . . . soon to be burned to a crisp, big brother. *(Pause)* Have you forgotten? We're never getting out of here alive. This is Xibalba. We can defeat death only by surrendering to it.

HUNAHPU: The fire pit?

[TECOLOTE enters.]

IXBALANQUE: Right. There's Tecolote. Maybe she can help us. *(Calling)* Oye, Tecolote!

HUNAHPU: Will you help us, Teco?

TECOLOTE: I don't see that I can. Your deaths have already been divined.

IXBALANQUE: But not the matter of our bodies' disposal.

TECOLOTE: I don't understand.

IXBALANQUE: The manner in which our bones are disposed will determine if we are to see the next life.

TECOLOTE: What about the Lords?

IXBALANQUE: They will do as you suggest.

TECOLOTE: You think so?

IXBALANQUE: I know so. *(IXBALANQUE whispers in her ear.)*

TECOLOTE: Your bones. . . ! The river. . . !

HUNAHPU: Yes!

TECOLOTE: I will try. *(With resolve)* I will take care of your remains.

IXBALANQUE: Good. We will keep our mother's promise to you, Teco.
You shall preside as guardian of the night throughout the forests of
Uleu.

[*THE LORDS can be heard entering.*]

BLOOD SAUSAGE: Boys! Oh boys!

[*TECOLOTE puts on her owl-servant face.*]

PATRIARCHAL PUS: *(To LOS GEMELOS)* Come my sons! Come see
what delicious meats we have cooked up for you!

BLOOD SAUSAGE: Yes, you must be famished after so much ball-playing.

[*LOS GEMELOS eye each other knowingly.*]

HUNAHPU: Ya con la mentiras, Viejos. No somos pendejos!

BLOOD SAUSAGE: But aren't you hungry?

IXBALANQUE: It is the mouth of that fire pit that is hungry for us.

[*LOS GEMELOS race up to the top of the pyramid, which is now
the edge of the fire pit. Lighting effects. They turn to each other,
wrap their arms around each other.*]

IXBALANQUE: Como cuates . . .

HUNAHPU: Y hermanos eternos, we enter and exit this world. *(They dive head-first into the oven.)*

PATRIARCHAL PUS: What Fools! Finally, the little bastards are out of sight!

BLOOD SAUSAGE: Let's celebrate! *(Music. THE LORDS begin to dance with each other.)*

TECOLOTE: *(Trying to get their attention)* Lords! Sir Sausage, Sir Pus . . . ?

PATRIARCHAL PUS: *(The music suddenly stops)* What is it, Owl? Don't you know how to party?

TECOLOTE: Their death is not complete, your Lordships, until there is no trace of their remains.

BLOOD SAUSAGE: The Owl speaks truly.

TECOLOTE: I overheard the twins saying that the fate they feared most was to have their bones ground down into the finest of flour and sprinkled as ashy dust into the river. There, you see, their death will be complete and their sleep eternal.

BLOOD SAUSAGE: So be it! Keep checking the barbeque, Owl. When the boys are thoroughly cooked, we will follow your recommendation exactly.

[THE LORDS exit. Crossfade to IXQUIC and IXMUCANE entering. They sit by the two corn plants.]

IXMUCANE: You have cried now, Daughter, for five days.

IXQUIC: And still I have rivers of tears inside me.

IXMUCANE: In the womb of that river, your sons are reborn, their ribs forming from the sculpted sands beneath the water. *(Indicating the plants)* Mira.

IXQUIC: I see green leaves sprouting from once-withered stalks.

IXMUCANE: Your tears have watered these plants.

IXQUIC: Let us give thanks. Our sons live!

[The plants dance. The WOMEN exit, dancing.]

Scene Eleven

[Music: "Carnaval." LOS GEMELOS enter wearing catfish faces, their clothes in tatters. They do a little dance.]

HUNAHPU: Step right up, Damas y Caballeros! Come witness for yourselves the greatest, most thrilling magic show in the world . . .

IXBALANQUE: Or should we say, the underworld.

HUNAHPU: We are magicians of the highest caliber . . .

IXBALANQUE: Trained by the University of Life . . .

HUNAHPU: And Death.

[THE LORDS OF DEATH enter.]

BLOOD SAUSAGE: Enough talk and self-congratulation.

PATRIARCHAL PUS: Start the show!

[HUNAHPU produces an obsidian blade.]

HUNAHPU: Is this more what you had in mind, Sirs?

PATRIARCHAL PUS: Ahhhh!

BLOOD SAUSAGE: Exactly!

IXBALANQUE: We now present a death-defying feat.

PATRIARCHAL PUS: But no one can defy the obsidian blade!

IXBALANQUE: We need a volunteer.

[They come down into the audience.]

HUNAHPU: A volunteer?

BLOOD SAUSAGE: Take that insolent owl!

TECOLOTE: Me? But what would you magicians want with me?

HUNAHPU: To remove your heart and put it back again.

IXBALANQUE: Alive!

PATRIARCHAL PUS: Impossible!

TECOLOTE: But it is a mere bird's heart.

BLOOD SAUSAGE: Oh, quit hesitating, you coward!

[THE LORDS push TECOLOTE over to the sacrificial site.]

TECOLOTE: You will return my heart alive, you say?

IXBALANQUE: It won't miss a beat.

[LOS GEMELOS lay TECOLOTE down, breast to the heavens. HUNAHPU raises the blade above his head. The crowd lets out a gasp. And HUNAHPU comes down with all his force into the feathered breast of TECOLOTE. IXBALANQUE digs his hands in and pulls out the beating heart.]

BLOOD SAUSAGE: Ah yes, a marvelous excavation!

PATRIARCHAL PUS: And done with such gusto! Might we not have a taste while it still pulses . . . ?

HUNAHPU: This heart is to be restored into the breast of the bird.

PATRIARCHAL PUS: Who ever heard of such a thing!

BLOOD SAUSAGE: Brother, if these vagabond clowns can return the life to this worthless owl. I will be the next to expose my breast to the magician's blade.

PATRIARCHAL PUS: And I will follow.

BLOOD SAUSAGE: On with the show!

IXBALANQUE: And now to resurrect the life of this bird . . . !

> [*LOS GEMELOS breathe upon TECOLOTE's beating heart and
> place it reverently back into her chest. They fill the gash in her breast
> with feathers and wait for a sign of life. Within a moment,
> TECOLOTE sits up, a full and complete owl.*]

IXBALANQUE: How do you feel?

TECOLOTE: Well, my plumas are a little ruffled. *(Applause)*

PATRIARCHAL PUS: Me next! Step aside, you feathered fool.

BLOOD SAUSAGE: No, me next! *(Pushes PATRIARCHAL PUS aside,
approaches the sacrificial site.)*

PATRIARCHAL PUS: *(A bit insulted)* Well!

HUNAHPU: How 'bout your head instead?

BLOOD SAUSAGE: My pleasure!

PATRIARCHAL PUS: *(Overlapping)* Why, even better!

> [*BLOOD SAUSAGE lays his head down upon the sacrificial table.
> HUNAHPU decapitates him. A sudden silence falls over the crowd as
> BLOOD SAUSAGE's head rolls onto the ground. LOS GEMELOS
> turn to PATRIARCHAL PUS.*]

PATRIARCHAL PUS: My turn! My turn! *(He rushes to the sacrificial site,
starts to lay his head down for decapitation, stops.)* Now, you're sure
this will work . . . ?

HUNAHPU: Absolutely!

> [*HUNAHPU pushes PATRIARCHAL PUS's head down onto
> the sacrificial table. IXBALANQUE chops it off. The Lords of Death
> have been vanquished. LOS GEMELOS break out into a dance,*]

holding the heads in the air. TECOLOTE joins them. Music: "Tecolote." Then she takes flight out of Xibalba forever. LOS GEMELOS watch her depart. Lighting transition. Moonlight. Music: "Los Cielos." IXQUIC appears at the top of the pyramid as la luna creciente.]

IXQUIC: Hijos. Do you recognize your mother?

LOS GEMELOS: We do. *(They meet her at the top of the pyramid. She puts headdresses on them. They become the sun and the moon.)*

IXQUIC: Sons, you are transformed. No longer earthly bodies, but celestial in nature. You, Hunahpu, the one star brilliant enough to be visible at the day's zenith. And you, Ixbalanque, the guardian of the night, visible once a month en la luna's full female face. We name you Sun and Moon.

IXBALANQUE: And you, Mamá, are named by la luna's changing aspects.

HUNAHPU: Waning moon. Waxing moon. El lado oscuro de la luna.

IXQUIC: *(Pause, the Music rises)* Let us go now. Your siblings, the Four Hundred Stars await us.

[Lighting transition. IXQUIC and LOS GEMELOS descend the pyramid and exit. Music fades out.]

Scene Twelve

[IXMUCANE enters, carrying the four humans in the shape of corn dolls. She is covered with the dust of corn flour.]

IXMUCANE: *(Calling out)* ¡Qué maravilla! ¡Qué maravilla! Miren, I think I've done it! This morning may be the dawn of humankind. Viejo! Kukulcan! *(CUCUMATZ and IXPIYACOC enter excitedly.)*

IXPIYACOC: Why, they're human beings!

CUCUMATZ: ¿Cómo lo hiciste, comadre?

IXMUCANE: The water became their blood, the corn their flesh. And the oil from my hands, as I worked them, became their muscle and fat.

[The DANCERS enter. IXMUCANE passes out the CORN PEOPLE to them in a ritualized fashion. The GODS ascend the pyramid and chant.]

Ch i biih na q'ut/Ri qa bi.
K oh i q'aharizah, oh i chuch,/Oh i qahav.

[Music/percussion. The CORN PEOPLE dance and praise their creators.]

DANCER: Corazón del Cielo.

DANCER: Heart of the Sky.

DANCER: Plumed Serpent.

DANCER: Huracan.

IXPIYACOC: They honor our names!

CUCUMATZ: At last! And so we pass onto you first humans, of the male and female kind, the project of humanity.

IXMUCANE: La raíz del tribu maya.

IXPIYACOC: Each with his own tongue, her own land.

CUCUMATZ: Multiply and become numerous, occupy the north and the south . . .

IXPIYACOC: The highlands and the low.

IXMUCANE: But remember always, to lift your faces to the sky.

[THE CORN PEOPLE dance and call out the names of the first peoples.]

DANCER: Balam Acab, Tigre de la Noche

DANCER: Chomihá, Agua Hermosa y Escogida

DANCER: Iquí Balam, Tigre de la Luna

DANCER: Caquixahá, Agua de Guacamaya

>   *[THE GODS and the CORN PEOPLE join together dancing and chanting.]*

ALL:
>   ucah tzucuxic
>   ucah xucutaxic
>   retaxic,
>   ucah cheexic,
>
>   umeh camaxic,
>   uyuc camaxic
>
>   upa cah,
>   upa uleu
>
>   cah tzuc
>   cah xucut

>   *[They exit. Silence. Only IXMUCANE remains on stage. She removes her headdress and once again becomes the DAYKEEPER.]*

DAYKEEPER: From these men and these women we are descended . . . Los Quichés. *(Pause)* And we turn our faces up to the sky and toward the Eastern place where the sun is born and give thanks.

This is the root de la Palabra Anciana. Are, u xe 'oher tzih.

>   *[She bows ceremoniously. The lights fade to black.]*

End of Play

Afterword

Homecoming:

The Politics of Myth and Location in Cherríe L. Moraga's
The Hungry Woman: A Mexican Medea
and *Heart of the Earth: A Popol Vuh Story*

Irma Mayorga

> *[A storyteller] assumes responsibility for his words, for what is
> created at the level of his human voice. He runs the risk of language,
> and language is full of risk. . . . His function is essentially creative,
> inasmuch as language is essentially creative. He creates himself, and
> his listeners, through the power of his perception, his imagination,
> his expression . . . he believes in the efficacy of words.*
> —N. Scott Momaday, "To Save a Great Vision"[1]

The homecoming Cherríe Moraga's plays give to Chicana/os is geographic,
psychic, decolonized, pre-Hispanic, and mythological in scope. In the case of
The Hungry Woman: A Mexican Medea and *Heart of the Earth: A Popol Vuh
Story,* the recovery of pre-Columbian myths serves as the conduit for cultural
critique and transformation. Myths are simultaneously sacred truths and symbolic metaphors, illuminating and mysterious, fiction and history, safe-guarded
and public, newly fashioned or of ancient origin, fantastical and quotidian;
and, they often escape the opposition of these binaries. But, most importantly,
myths are stories. In Western theatre, stories are the province of playwrights.
For Moraga's Chicana dramaturgy, the staging of pre-Columbian
Mesoamerican myths serves not only as a way to reignite Chicana/o collective
consciousness and foster paths towards cultural affirmation, but also as vi-
able means through which the legacies of patriarchy, homophobia, and
xenophobic nationalisms can be counteracted with feminist visions and queer
perspectives of the "near future."[2]

Moraga began work on *The Hungry Woman: A Mexican Medea* in the
early 1990s and continued to develop the play throughout the writing and
publication of her books *The Last Generation* (1992) and *Waiting in the Wings*

(1997); therefore, the play resonates with ideas, themes, and events contained in these two works. In terms of playwriting, Moraga continually searches for ways to enlist the theatre to elucidate her socio-political location as a Chicana, a lesbian, and a feminist. As such, the conversation that evolves between Moraga's creative non-fiction and poetry and her dramatic projects should always be considered a primary relationship: her dramatic works consistently take up and give new dimension to the themes of her non-fiction.

The Hungry Woman: A Mexican Medea constructs a gripping crosscut between the mexicana/o legend of La Llorona, the pre-Columbian myth of the dismemberment of the moon deity Coyolxauhqui, and the Greek myth of Medea. Moraga connects the betrayals and desires these women suffer to the Aztec creation myth of The Hungry Woman, a woman with mouths all over her body and an insatiable hunger whom the Aztec gods Quetzalcoatl and Tezcatlipoca drag down from the spirit realm and break in two, transforming her halves into the bounty of the earth and the blanket of the sky. Yet she still cries out in hunger.[3] For Moraga, the link between mythic figures such as La Llorona, Coyolxauhqui, and the Aztec Hungry Woman is a seminal one:

> *And at last, upon encountering this myth—this pre-capitalist, pre-colonial, pre-catholic mito—my jornada began to make sense. This is the original Llorona y tiene mucha hambre. I realized that she has been the subject of my work all along, from my earliest writings, my earliest feminism. She is the story that has never been told truly, the story of that hungry Mexican woman who is called puta/bruja/jota/loca because she refuses to forget that her half-life is not a natural-born fact.[4]*

In the myths of these broken and maligned women, Moraga sees the state of all Chicanas/mexicanas who suffer the legacy of their antepasados in the injustices of patriarchy. For her playwriting, allowing these women to speak—to attain voices and objectives beyond the confinement of myths tooled to service patriarchy—becomes the point of departure for drama that inspires hunger for empowerment.

The Hungry Woman incorporates some of Moraga's most challenging and imaginative stage elements yet conceived in her playwriting: all roles are played by female actors except for Chac-mool, Medea's twelve-year-old son; the play utilizes Aztec dance and gesture, mythological figures, and perceptions of time to render a deromanticized representation of the Aztec cosmos, thereby remetaphorizing the indigenous underpinnings Chicanismo depends upon; Moraga conflates geopolitical "border crossings" with the Catholic rite of confession to render the interanimations between physical and cultural transgressions within a geography of Chicana/o space and psyche; scenes of explicit lesbian sexuality illustrate the relationship between the desire to emancipate sexuality and the roots of political resistance; and, the play revolves around the topic of infanticide.

For the most part, *The Hungry Woman's* story and structure follows the Euripidean tragedy of Medea. Specifically, it retains the trope of the fallen woman and the driving principle of autochthony, which Euripides's tragedy interrogated for his Athenian spectators. To fashion a Chicana/o translation, Moraga's tragedy places emphasis on the ancient northern homeland of the Aztec people, Aztlán.

Like many Chicana/o writers and thinkers before her, Moraga turns to the culturally organizing image of Aztlán to structure her ideas: "Aztlán gave language to a nameless anhelo inside me."[5] Aztlán is an important physical and psychic point of origin for Chicana/o peoples.[6] In the tradition of its mythology, Aztlán was believed to have been located somewhere in what is now the U.S. Southwest (formerly northern Mexico before the 1848 Treaty of Guadalupe Hidalgo). The Aztecs migrated from Aztlán to central Mexico in approximately 1168 A.D.[7] Seminal documents generated in the energies of the Chicano Movement such as "El Plan Espiritual de Aztlán" (1969) seized upon the political and spiritual fecundity of Aztlán to shape the foundation of Chicano oppositional resistance and cultural nationalism: " 'El Plan Espiritual de Aztlán' sets the theme that Chicanos . . . must use their nationalism as the key or common denominator for mass mobilization and organization."[8] Chicano Nationalist claims along these lines exposed the artificiality of the geo-political border between the U.S. and Mexico and repositioned Mexican-descended peoples of the U.S. not as "illegal aliens" in U.S. held lands, but rather, the land's original indigenous inhabitants. This land-based oppositional strategy emblematizes social theory concerning subjugation and space, as cultural geographer Edward Soja writes: "We must be insistently aware of how space can be made to hide consequences from us, how relations of power and discipline are inscribed into the apparently innocent spatiality of social life, how human geographies become filled with politics and ideology."[9]

In the Movement's era, the concept of Aztlán—an indigenous homeland inside the U.S.—helped bolster the idea of a Chicano sovereignty: a Native claim to Southwest lands seized by the U.S. from Mexico. Aztlán inverts the hegemonic narrative of "Manifest Destiny" and provides a new lens of ethnic consciousness for Chicano civil rights. In *Chicano Poetics: Heterotexts and Hybridities*, poet/scholar Alfred Arteaga describes the importance of this tactical reorientation: "To be a Chicano and to live in Aztlán is to have historical precedence over Anglos in the Southwest. . . . Chicanos descend historically from Indians."[10] While conquest produces the racially mixed mestizo body (part European and part Indian) and U.S. colonization produces differential national identities, the linchpin of Indianness vis-à-vis Aztlán serves as the pathway to alternative paradigms of Chicano subjectivity and self-determination. Chicano nationalist ideology depends upon the element of Indianness as a crucial component for inspiring resistant collective action.

However, Chicano cultural nationalism also cultivated monolithic and static definitions of the Native roots which grounded its program. As Moraga observes in her analysis, "For a generation, nationalist leaders used a kind of 'selective memory,' drawing exclusively from those aspects of Mexican and Native cultures that served the interests of male heterosexuals. At times, they took the worst of Mexican machismo and Aztec warrior bravado, combined it with some of the most oppressive male-conceived idealizations of 'traditional' Mexican womanhood and called that cultural integrity."[11] Chicanismo's failure to acknowledge the intra-cultural diversity of Chicana/o identities (differences based on region, gender, class, language, and sexuality), along with internally antagonistic factions in the Movement, eventually dissolved the cohesion Aztlán initially inspired.

As Chicana historian Alma García offers, Chicanismo of any type similar to the strident social movement of the 1960s and early 1970s is diffused by the 1980s—"The Decade of the Hispanic."[12] However, post-Movement Chicana feminists of Moraga's generation inherit the unfinished political projects begun by women and men in the height of the Movement. Along with her Chicana feminist contemporaries, Moraga gathers the remnants of the Movement's ideas for her own feminist, lesbian, and cultural ends to begin constructing a new form of Chicanismo:

> *Chicanos are an occupied nation within a nation, and women*
> *and women's sexuality are occupied within the Chicano nation.*
> *If women's bodies and those of men and women who transgress*
> *their gender roles have been historically regarded as territories to*
> *be conquered, they are also territories to be liberated. Feminism*
> *has taught us this. The nationalism I seek is one that decolonizes*
> *the brown and female body as it decolonizes the brown and*
> *female earth.*[13]

By the 1990s, Moraga's ideological vision foments in *The Last Generation,* most specifically in her essay "Queer Aztlán: The Re-formation of Chicano Tribe," which contains the heart of her theoretical ideas for assembling an egalitarian, consciously indigenous Chicana/o future. The attainment of a Native future is contingent on dismantling the problematic form of indigenismo invoked in the heyday of the Movement. The horizon of her vision includes amplifying the linkages between Chicana/os' disenfranchisements to the struggles of indigenous peoples throughout the world: "If the material basis of every nationalist move-ment is land, then the reacquisition, defense, and protection of Native land and its natural resources are the basis for rebuilding Chicano nation."[14]

Focus on Chicano Nationalism's exclusionary practices and Aztlán's symbolic currency organizes *The Hungry Woman's* setting and plot in impor-tant ways. The play unfolds within an ensemble of four spaces: Aztlán, a heteronormative, patriarchally structured "Chicano country"; Gringolandia, "Anglo country"; Phoenix, Arizona, now called Tamoanchán, a policed "res-ervation" on the border between Aztlán and Gringolandia populated by jotería, undesirable "poisons" to the status quo of heteronormativity in Aztlán, as well as other queer peoples of color; and, a mythical realm inhabited by a spirit chorus of Aztec warrior women—the Cihuatateo—mothers who have died in childbirth. Aztlán arises from a "balkanization" of the U.S. nation-state as the result of civil war, which yields separate countries for different racial groups. This delineation of spaces theatrically mimics the cultural bound-aries of gender, sexuality, politics, and myth for Chicana/os. The characters travel among the spaces: their individual journeys catalogue the price of trans-gressing "borders," creating a visual and theatrical cognitive mapping of Chicana/o cultural divisions that impede attainment of Chicanismo.

Medea, a curandera and midwife, has fought hard as a rebel in the play's fictionalized revolution to help achieve Aztlán. Now, she despises patriarchy's deformation of Aztlán's governance. As the play opens, Medea lies incarcerated in the psychiatric ward of a prison, an interstitial place in neither Aztlán's nor Phoenix's borders. She has killed her son Chac-mool to prevent his indoctrination into Aztlán's misogyny and machismo. We gain her story through retrospective structure as she narrates the past seven years of events. Medea was once the wife of Jasón, a poet and high-ranking leader of the new Chicano country. He discovers his wife's "illegal" lesbian relation-ship with Luna, a Chicana sculptor and stone mason. Medea's consciousness as a political revolutionary has reshaped her emotional and sexual desire: "It was the most natural evolution in the world to move from love of country to love of you [Luna]" (p. 80). Betraying her marriage to Jasón and her "proper" role as a woman forces Medea into exile; she takes Chac-mool to join Luna in the jotería-populated Phoenix.

Jasón's position in and with regard to Aztlán is no less problematic than Medea's. Jasón lacks the crucial percentile of "Native" blood required for citizenship in the Chicano country: "You can't hold onto a handful of dirt in Aztlán without him [Chac-mool]. You don't have the blood quantum" (p. 72), declares the indígena mexicana Medea. True to "El Plan Espiritual de Aztlán's" agenda, the new Aztlán has resorted to indigenous measures of au-thenticity: "the call of our blood is our power."[15] To meet this requirement of authenticity and move forward his ambitions, Jasón plans to marry a young india, but he discovers his new bride is barren. Therefore, he comes to Medea in Phoenix to demand custody of Chac-mool. Jasón intends to use his only child as a pawn in his political ascension.

Chac-mool, the "messenger between this world and the other" in the Aztec religion, will soon be thirteen, an age that permits him to leave exile in Phoenix and partake in ceremonies that will indoctrinate him into Aztlán's construction of masculinity. Yet Medea has worked to rear her son into a new type of man: one who admonishes the hate Chicanas/os harbor for the jotería and recognizes the oppressions exerted upon women. Caught between the need to define the terms of his masculinity and love for his mother, Chac-mool's choices present the boy with no means to mediate respect for his mother's feminist beliefs and Chicano "manhood." Instead, Chac-mool argues he can return to Aztlán and change the terms of masculinity the country prescribes. However, Medea insists he will fail in his efforts to eradicate the deep roots of patriarchy and homophobia and, eventually, betray their bond. On the eve of his departure, Medea takes the life of her child.

Euripides' tragedy ends with the flight of Medea to Athens, the bodies of her two dead children gathered into a chariot she rides provided by the Sun god Apollo. Moraga's ending also provides a redemptive rescue by the "son." Rather than abandon her protagonist in the confinement of Aztlán's governance, Luna and Chac-mool aid in Medea's strategic recovery. Luna brings herbs that will end Medea's life and, thus, imprisonment; likewise, the spirit of Chac-mool returns to his mother's side. He has come to guide her to a home beyond the confines of the earth where she has neither land nor country.

The Hungry Woman: A Mexican Medea functions as a prophetic cautionary tale about the complexity of power. Moraga's consideration of intra-cultural oppressions based on gender and sexuality problematizes foundational narratives of Chicano Nationalist ideology in provocative ways even as her artistic production attends to the discourse of Aztlán's symbolic viability. Yet the play's ethos still resides within "El Plan's" desires for Chicana/o cultural production: "We must insure that our writers, poets, musicians, and artists produce literature and art that is appealing to our people and relates to our revolutionary culture."[16] Considering the crucial challenges the play throws up to Chicano masculinity, the gender scripts of Chicanas, sexuality, formations of family, and nationhood, it is perhaps not surprising that at the time of this printing Chicano and Latino theater companies find the work daunting and have yet to undertake producing the play. In a similar regard, the play's culturally specific conversations and concerns have also prevented its ability to interest mainstream (Euroamerican) theatre companies.

While *The Hungry Woman* draws creative resources from Aztec cosmology and mythic traditions, *The Heart of the Earth: A Popol Vuh Story* delves into the mythic landscape of the Quiché Maya. Originally commissioned by the International Arts Relations (INTAR) Hispanic American Arts Center, *Heart of the Earth: A Popol Vuh Story* first premiered at The Public Theatre in New York on September 14, 1994 as part of the Jim Henson Foundation's International Festival of Puppet Theatre. *Heart of the Earth* also received production at The John F. Kennedy Center for the Performing Arts in January 1997. Collaboration with director and puppeteer Ralph Lee aided in the development of the final staged version of the play.

Moraga's adaptation dramatizes major events from the first four parts of the complicated Maya creation myth as recorded in the Mayan book, the *Popol Vuh*.[17] During the European conquest of the Maya in the sixteenth century, Spanish missionaries burned vast libraries of sophisticated Mayan hieroglyphic books; today, only four of the pre-conquest Mayan picture books exist.[18] However, in the eighteenth century, an alphabetic (non-hieroglyphic) version of the *Popol Vuh* surfaced in Chichicastenango, Guatemala, presumably written in secret shortly after the conquest by literate Quiché Maya. A Spanish friar, self-taught in the Quiché language, "happened to get a look at this manuscript" and transcribed the story into Spanish—the original text then disappeared back into the Guatemalan highlands.[19]

The Maya looked to the *Popol Vuh* as a "seeing instrument" or a "place to see" both past and future events.[20] As Dennis Tedlock explains, the ancient Maya not only read the *Popol Vuh* with an interpretive dimension, but on occasion, "daykeepers" (diviners "who know how to interpret illnesses, omens, dreams, messages . . . and the multiple rhythms of time") often gave "a long performance and account" in their oral interpretations of the world's creation by weaving the book's astronomical charts, pictures, plot outlines, and glyphs into story for an audience.[21] Daykeepers exist even today as learned and revered figures within Quiché Maya communities.[22] Moraga's theatrical transposition functions as a Chicana/o equivalent to the daykeeper's task: she, too, takes the many stories contained within the sacred book, reanimates their lessons and messages, and offers a new "performance" with insights pertinent to the context of our contemporary conditions.

Moraga's theatrical retelling incorporates a wide variety of languages including English, Spanish, Quiché, and other Mayan tongues, Spanglish, Chicano speech from the Southwest, and "the urban colloquialism of U.S. city streets" (p. 104). Reflective of Moraga's origins as a poet, the language of the play also features a strong poetic cadence, intertwining the many tongues she employs into a lyrical syncretism. While *Heart of the Earth* remains faithful to its Mayan origins, the patois combinations of the play's language demonstrates that the Quiché dialect of the Maya language is a living, not just ancient, form and its adaptation can incorporate the effects of a U.S. milieu: "The world of language I hope to evoke is one of a diverse and people-of-color América that more closely reflects its changing and beautifully darkening face as we enter the twenty-first century" (p.104). Like the Maya themselves, Moraga attunes her work to the rhythms of time's movement, past and present.

Heart of the Earth utilizes many creative elements to portray the mythological characters and phantasmagoric situations of the *Popol Vuh's* pre-human world. Chief among these elements is puppetry: puppets serve as the play's more fantastical figures, while other characters modulate from human form to puppet incarnations. The set features a large, Maya-style pyramid where much of the action takes place along its graduated tiers. At the pyramid's base, the tiers lengthen and widen to resemble plateaus the Maya carved into mountainsides for farming. Given this open setting, music and lighting suggest changes of locale, shifts in time, and signal recurring themes. In many scenes, Maya dance and gesture dramatizes actions related to reverence, conflict, trickery, or birth. The interspersion of chants in the Quiché tongue contributes a ceremonial aspect to the myth's dramatization.

Moraga's condensed version of the myth concentrates on the many births, deaths, and travails that the ancient god Ixpiyacoc (abuelo) and his goddess partner Ixmucane (abuela) endure in the raising of their twin sons—the Mayan heroes Hunahpu and Vucub. Cucumatz, the Maya's green, plumed-serpent god, is also prominently featured as a comic compadre of Ixpiyacoc. The play focuses on these ancient grandparents' attempts to first create the earth, Uleu, and the animals, and then mortal beings who will "praise their creators" in a proper fashion. The central event of the play traces the twin's journey to the Mayan underworld of Xibalba and their subsequent decapitations by Xibalba's cruel Lords, Patriarchal Pus and Blood Sausage. The Lords then have the head of Hunahpu placed in the limbs of a calabash tree as a warning to their ghostly subjects. Consequently, the calabash tree blossoms to life. Ixquic, the oppressed daughter of Patriarchal Pus, finds Hunahpu's talking head in the blossoming tree and becomes magically impregnated by his saliva. Patriarchal Pus and Blood Sausage detect Ixquic's life-giving state and, for this betrayal to the codes of Xibalba and her feminine honor, command their owl-servant Tecolote to kill her. Instead, Tecolote leads Ixquic to the world above Xibalba, saving her life and that of her children—a second set of twin brothers, Hunahpu (the second) and Ixbalanque. As the creation myth demands, this sequence of events is doomed to repeat itself, but each cyclical version brings the characters closer to the story's final resolution: the death of Xibalba's Lords and the birth of humankind. Upon completing the difficult task of defeating the underworld's masters, and sacrificing their own lives in the effort, the twins are rewarded by the gods who transform them into the earth's sun and moon, and Ixquic settles in the night sky between her sons, ever changing as the moon's waxing and waning phases.

In its world of magical transformations, speaking animals, and repetitious evolutions, the spirituality of the Mayan *Popol Vuh* gains a contemporary translation with Moraga's inclusion of distinctly Chicana/o details.

For example, satire and humor arises from the characters' self-reflexive lapses into cholo and pachuco mannerisms, flashes of Chicana/o historical consciousness, and pointed send-ups of competing creation narratives (p. 123):

> IXQUIC: But, Father, I have not known a man in the biblical sense.
> PATRICARCHAL PUS: This is not the bible. This is the *Popol Vuh*.

Social critique also finds form in Moraga's tale as the play includes allusions to the AIDS pandemic, questions the twins zealous devotion to their ball playing ("Trust your brain, not your brawn" [p. 116], warns Ixmucane), and features characters in pursuit of a place to call home.

Characteristic of her feminist voice as a playwright, Moraga foregrounds women's issues despite the *Heart of the Earth's* many male protagonists. The story of Ixquic's efforts to escape the destructive dominance of her father, Patriarchal Pus, provides an important feminist counterpoint to the twin's young bravado and heroic misadventures. In this stead, Moraga stresses Ixquic's alternative name, "Blood Woman." This naming enables Xibalba's hierarchy to represent the tensions of racial bias: the white ghosts of Xibalba ridicule and persecute Ixquic because of her dark, radiant color. Ixmucane also provides an opportunity for feminist perspectives. From behind her metate stone, Ixmucane comments on Ixpiyacoc's and the twin's foolish actions with sly reprimands and wise critiques. Once Ixmucane realizes that Ixquic carries the children of her son Hunahpu, the two women work in coalition to protect the young boys from repeating the fate of their father and uncle. Yet, these new twins must continue the *Popol Vuh's* cycle; they proceed into Xibalba. On earth, Ixmucane and Ixquic offer prayers for their return. Ixmucane also demonstrates to Cucumatz and Ixpiyacoc the shortcomings of their plans to build the first humans from mud or wood. In the end, she solves the dilemma of creating human life by fashioning mortals from the Mayan earth's best resource, maize.

Although *Heart of the Earth* has received its world premiere in New York, the work has yet to be produced in the many regions and locales that Chicana/os inhabit in substantial numbers. As such, the work remains unknown to the Mesoamerican descendents of its Mayan story. This new play volume serves as introduction and record keeper, enabling Moraga's storytelling as a Chicana playwright—a contemporary task consonant to the Aztec Tlamatinime and the Maya daykeeper—to help us "envision the map back to the original face" of Chicana/o origins, thereby informing the choices of our future.[23] In this, Cherríe Moraga's teatro draws its strength from the vast reservoir of cultural signifiers that structure the differences between Chicana/o dramaturgy and Euroamerican playwriting, reterritorializing the stage with a sense of place we can call home.

Endnotes

1. N. Scott Momaday, "To Save a Great Vision," in *The Man Made of Words: Essays, Stories, Passages* (New York, St. Martin's Press, 1997): 23.

2. The conceptual setting of *The Hungry Woman: A Mexican Medea.*

3. A full account of the The Hungry Woman story is contained in *The Hungry Woman: Myths and Legends of the Aztecs,* ed. John Bierhorst (New York: Quill/William Morrow, 1993): 23-25.

4. Cherríe Moraga, "Looking for the Insatiable Woman," in *Loving in the War Years: lo que nunca pasó por sus labios,* 2nd ed. (Cambridge: South End Press, 2000): 142-150.

5. Cherríe Moraga, "Queer Aztlán: The Re-formation of Chicano Tribe," in *The Last Generation* (Boston: South End Press, 1993): 150. The subject of Aztlán has generated a vast amount of Chicana/o literature and scholarly inquiry. A critical introduction to these writings is the diverse collection of essays gathered in *Aztlán: Essays on the Chicano Homeland,* eds. Rudolfo A. Anaya and Francis A. Lomelí (Albuquerque: University of New Mexico Press, 1989).

6. For a recent examination of Aztlán's mytho-historical formation and symbolic significance in terms of Mexican and Chicana/o identity, see Daniel Cooper Alarcón's essay "Toward a New Understanding of Aztlán and Chicano Cultural Identity," in *The Aztec Palimpsest: Mexico in the Modern Imagination* (Tucson: The University of Arizona Press, 1997): 3-35.

7. Alfred Arteaga, *Chicano Poetics: Heterotexts and Hybridities* (Cambridge: Cambridge University Press, 1997): 9.

8. "El Plan Espiritual de Aztlán," in *Aztlán: Essays on the Chicano Homeland,* eds. Rudolfo A. Anaya and Francisco Lomelí (Albuquerque: University of New Mexico Press, 1989): 1-5.

9. Edward Soja, *Postmodern Geographies: The Reassertion of Space in Critical Social Theory* (London: Verso, 1989): 25.

10. Arteaga, *Chicano Poetics,* 9.

11. Moraga, "Queer Aztlán," 156.

12. Alma M. García, ed., *Chicana Feminist Thought: The Basic Historical Writings* (London: Routledge, 1997): 261.

13. Moraga, "Queer Aztlán," 150. To name but a few, the writings of Chicana feminists such as Gloria Anzaldúa, Ana Castillo, Rosa Linda Fregosa, and Angie Chabram also seek to assess the Movement's fragmentation.

14. Moraga, "Queer Aztlán," 170.

15. "El Plan Espiritual de Aztlán," 1.

16. Ibid., 3.

17. "Introduction," in *Popol Vuh: The Sacred Book of the Ancient Quiché Maya*, eds. Delia Goetz and Sylvanus G. Morley, from the Spanish trans. by Adrián Recinos (Norman: The University of Oklahoma Press, 1950): 5. The *Popol Vuh* is also known as *The Book of the Council, Book of the Community,* or the *Sacred Book*.

18. Dennis Tedlock, trans., "Introduction," in *Popol Vuh: The Definitive Edition of the Mayan Book of the Dawn of Life and the Glories of Gods and Kings* (New York: Simon and Schuster, 1985): 27.

19. Tedlock, "Introduction," 28. For a more complete account of the *Popol Vuh's* enigmatic post-conquest history, see the "Introduction" to both citations above.

20 Tedlock, "Introduction," 32.

21. Tedlock, "Introduction," 32-3.

22. Tedlock, "Introduction," 13-15. In his "Preface," Tedlock gives credit to a Quiché Mayan daykeeper whom he often consulted with in the effort to generate a new English language version of the *Popol Vuh*.

23. Moraga, "Queer Aztlán," 187.